HARCOURT
Science

Harcourt School Publishers

Orlando • Boston • Dallas • Chicago • San Diego

www.harcourtschool.com

Cover Image
This butterfly is a Red Cracker. It is almost completely red on its underside. It is called a cracker because the males make a crackling sound as they fly. The Red Cracker is found in Central and South America.

Printed in the United States of America

ISBN 0-15-315686-4	UNIT A
ISBN 0-15-315687-2	UNIT B
ISBN 0-15-315688-0	UNIT C
ISBN 0-15-315689-9	UNIT D
ISBN 0-15-315690-2	UNIT E
ISBN 0-15-315691-0	UNIT F

2 3 4 5 6 7 8 9 10 032 2000

Authors

Marjorie Slavick Frank
Former Adjunct Faculty Member at Hunter, Brooklyn, and Manhattan Colleges
New York, New York

Robert M. Jones
Professor of Education
University of Houston-Clear Lake
Houston, Texas

Gerald H. Krockover
Professor of Earth and Atmospheric Science Education
School Mathematics and Science Center
Purdue University
West Lafayette, Indiana

Mozell P. Lang
Science Education Consultant
Michigan Department of Education
Lansing, Michigan

Joyce C. McLeod
Visiting Professor
Rollins College
Winter Park, Florida

Carol J. Valenta
Vice President—Education, Exhibits, and Programs
St. Louis Science Center
St. Louis, Missouri

Barry A. Van Deman
Science Program Director
Arlington, Virginia

UNIT B

LIFE SCIENCE

Plants and Animals Interact

UNIT C

EARTH SCIENCE
Earth's Land

EARTH SCIENCE
Cycles on Earth and In Space

UNIT E

PHYSICAL SCIENCE
Investigating Matter

UNIT F

PHYSICAL SCIENCE
Exploring Energy and Forces

Using Science Process Skills

When scientists try to find an answer to a question or do an experiment, they use thinking tools called process skills. You use many of the process skills whenever you think, listen, read, and write. Think about how these students used process skills to help them answer questions and do experiments.

Maria is interested in birds. She carefully observes the birds she finds. Then she uses her book to identify the birds and learn more about them.

Try This Find something outdoors that you want to learn more about. Use your senses to observe it carefully.

Talk About It What senses does Maria use to observe the birds?

Process Skills

Observe—use your senses to learn about objects and events

Charles finds rocks for a rock collection. He observes the rocks he finds. He compares their colors, shapes, sizes, and textures. He classifies them into groups according to their colors.

Try This Use the skills of comparing and classifying to organize a collection of objects.

Talk About It What other ways can Charles classify the rocks in his collection?

Process Skills

Compare — identify characteristics of things or events to find out how they are alike and different

Classify — group or organize objects or events in categories based on specific characteristics

Katie measures her plants to see how they grow from day to day. Each day after she **measures** she **records the data**. Recording the data will let her work with it later. She **displays the data** in a graph.

Try This Find a shadow in your room. Measure its length each hour. Record your data, and find a way to display it.

Talk About It How does displaying your data help you communicate with others?

Process Skills

Measure — compare mass, length, or capacity of an object to a unit, such as gram, centimeter, or liter

Record Data — write down observations

Display Data — make tables, charts, or graphs

An ad about low-fat potato chips claims that low-fat chips have half the fat of regular potato chips. Tani **plans and conducts an investigation** to test the claim.

Tani labels a paper bag Regular and Low-Fat. He finds two chips of each kind that are the same size, and places them above their labels. He crushes all the chips flat against the bag. He sets the stopwatch for one hour.

Tani **predicts** that regular chips will make larger grease spots on the bag than low-fat chips. When the stopwatch signals, he checks the spots. The spots above the Regular label are larger than the spots above the Low-Fat label. Tani **infers** that the claim is correct.

Try This Plan and conduct an investigation to test claims for a product. Make a prediction, and tell what you infer from the results.

Talk About It Why did Tani test potato chips of the same size?

Process Skills

Plan and conduct investigations— identify and perform the steps necessary to find the answer to a question

Predict— form an idea of an expected outcome based on observations or experience

Infer— use logical reasoning to explain events and make conclusions

You will have many opportunities to practice and apply these and other process skills in *Harcourt Science*. An exciting year of science discoveries lies ahead!

Safety in Science

Here are some safety rules to follow.

1. Think ahead. Study the steps and safety symbols of the investigation so you know what to expect. If you have any questions, ask your teacher.

2. Be neat. Keep your work area clean. If you have long hair, pull it back so it doesn't get in the way. Roll up long sleeves. If you should spill or break something, or get cut, tell your teacher right away.

3. Watch your eyes. Wear safety goggles when told to do so.

4. Yuck! Never eat or drink anything during a science activity unless you are told to do so by your teacher.

5. Don't get shocked. Be sure that electric cords are in a safe place where you can't trip over them. Don't ever pull a plug out of an outlet by pulling on the cord.

6. Keep it clean. Always clean up when you have finished. Put everything away and wash your hands.

In some activities you will see these symbols. They are signs for what you need to do to be safe.

CAUTION
Be especially careful.

CAUTION
Wear safety goggles.

CAUTION
Be careful with sharp objects.

CAUTION
Don't get burned.

CAUTION
Protect your clothes.

CAUTION
Protect your hands with mitts.

CAUTION
Be careful with electricity.

Cycles on Earth and in Space

Unit Project ## Sky Observations

Plan a schedule for recording sky observations for one
month. Make daily notes about the weather including
temperature, precipitation, and cloud formations. If you
like, add a weekly weather map. Sketch the appearance of
the moon each night. At the end of the month, review
your notes and describe the cycles you see.

Vocabulary Preview

groundwater
estuary
evaporation
condensation
precipitation
water cycle

The Water Cycle

There's plenty of water on Earth. In fact, Earth is nearly covered with it. Most of the water on Earth is frozen or salty. And even though water seems to be everywhere, in some places on Earth there is almost no water at all.

FAST FACT

A leaky faucet wastes about 76 liters (20 gal) of water a day. If you wait a week to fix the leak, the faucet will drip 800,000 drops!

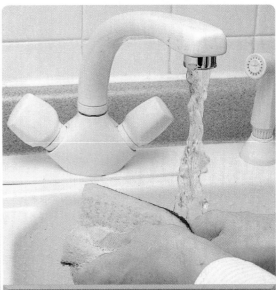

How Much Water

Activity	Liters
Brushing teeth for two minutes	23
Running a dishwasher	45
Shower	95
Washing a load of laundry	190

It takes 159,000 liters (42,000 gal) of water to grow and prepare the food for a Thanksgiving dinner for eight people. That's enough water to fill a swimming pool!

Where Is Water Found on Earth?

In this lesson, you can . . .

INVESTIGATE
how much water covers Earth's surface.

LEARN ABOUT
why water is important to living things.

LINK to math, writing, art, and technology.

INVESTIGATE

Land or Water

Activity Purpose Does Earth's surface have more land or more water? In this investigation you will play a game to **collect data** about Earth's surface. Then you will **use numbers** to estimate the amount of water on Earth's surface.

Materials
- plastic inflatable globe

Activity Procedure

1 Work in groups of five. Choose one person to be the recorder. The other four people will toss the ball.

2 Have the four ball tossers stand in a circle. The recorder hands the ball to the first person, who gently tosses the ball to another person in the circle. (Picture A)

◄ If you live in a cold place, you may see water in the form of snow.

3 The catcher should catch the ball with open hands. Check to see if the tip of the catcher's right index finger is on land or water. The recorder should **record** this data.

4 Continue tossing and recording until the ball has been tossed 20 times.

5 Repeat Steps 3 and 4 two more times.

Picture A

Draw Conclusions

1. Total your counts. How many times did the catcher's right index finger touch water? Touch land?

2. Where did the catchers' fingers land more often? Why do you think so?

3. **Scientists at Work** Scientists **use numbers** to **collect data.** Using your data, estimate how much of Earth's surface is covered by water.

Investigate Further You did this investigation 3 times. The more data you collect, the better your data becomes. How would doing the investigation 10 times change your data? Try it to find out.

Process Skill Tip

Collecting data by **using numbers** can help you answer questions. By doing the activity several times, you increase the amount of data you collect. Then you can **interpret the data** to find an answer to your question.

This view of Earth from space makes it easy to see why Earth is sometimes called the water planet. ▶

Water on Earth

FIND OUT

- why water is important
- where water is found on Earth

VOCABULARY

groundwater
estuary

The Importance of Water

From space, Earth looks like a blue marble. The water that covers most of the planet makes it look blue. Earth's lands are really small islands in the middle of huge oceans and seas.

Without water there could be no life on Earth. Plants and animals need water to live. So do people. Two-thirds of your body is water. People must have at least 2 liters (about 2 qt) of water each day to survive. Even the foods you eat are full of water. Chicken is three-fourths water. A potato is four-fifths water.

Water is important to Earth's environment. Without water there could be no rain or snow. Water helps make winds and storms. Water even changes the shape of Earth's surface.

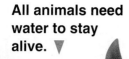
All animals need water to stay alive. ▼

▲ Industry uses about half of our fresh water. Water is used to wash things, to cool things down, and to make products.

Look at a map of Earth. You can see that most water on Earth is found in the oceans. This water is salt water. Many plants and animals live in the ocean. But salt water isn't good for the plants and animals that live on land or in fresh water.

Living things on land need fresh water. Only a little of Earth's water is fresh water. But not all the fresh water can be used. Most fresh water is frozen as ice in glaciers or in icecaps near the poles. Only a small amount of Earth's fresh water can be used to meet the needs of living things.

✔ **What are the two types of water on Earth?**

▲ Irrigation is the moving of water to dry places. Irrigation helps plants grow in dry areas. Almost two-fifths of Earth's liquid fresh water is used for irrigation.

Water on Earth

 Fresh Water

 Ice

If you could put all the water on Earth into 100 buckets, 97 buckets would hold the salt water of the oceans and seas, and 2 buckets would hold the frozen fresh water of glaciers and icecaps. Only 1 bucket would hold liquid fresh water.

Salt Water

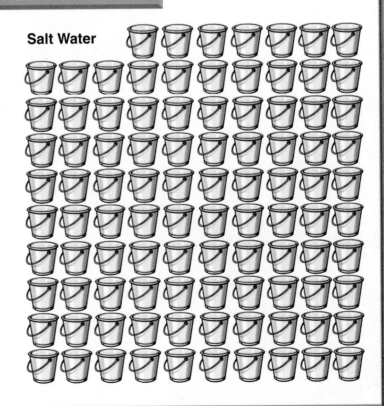

Fresh Water

Nearly every person in the United States uses more than 380 liters (about 100 gal) of fresh water every day. You use fresh water when you take a drink. You take baths in fresh water. You water your plants with fresh water. You cook with fresh water. Farmers grow your food with fresh water. Factories use fresh water to make everything from bread to steel. People find the fresh water they need in many places. The rain or snow that falls to Earth is fresh water. This water flows over the ground and into rivers and streams. Ponds and most lakes also hold fresh water.

There is also fresh water under Earth's surface. This water is called **groundwater**. Groundwater begins as rain soaking into the soil. The water moves down through the soil and broken rocks under the soil until it reaches solid rock. Much of Earth's fresh water is stored underground as groundwater.

Fresh water is not found evenly on Earth's surface. Some places have a great deal of fresh water. Other places have very little. In those places there may not be enough water to meet the needs of the people who live there. In some places pollution makes the water dirty. Polluted water cannot be used by people.

◀ Most of Earth's fresh water is frozen. Glaciers and icecaps cover one-tenth of Earth's land surface. This iceberg has broken away from a glacier and is floating in the ocean.

To make sure there is enough clean, fresh water for everyone, it is important to conserve, or save, water when you can. Take short showers. Turn off the water when you brush your teeth. And don't pour paints, oils, or other harmful liquids down the drain. These liquids can get into the water people drink and make it unhealthful.

✔ **Where is fresh water found on Earth?**

Water on Earth

Water that falls on the Earth collects in lakes, ponds, rivers, and streams.

Snow falls in cold areas.

The water from melted snow flows into streams and ponds.

Rain soaks into soil and rock. It becomes groundwater.

Some water from rain goes into rivers and streams.

Some water is stored in ponds and lakes.

Sometimes groundwater rises to the surface to form a lake.

Salt Water

Earth is a watery planet. Much of that water is salt water. The salt water of Earth's oceans covers more than two-thirds of our planet's surface. The Pacific Ocean is Earth's largest ocean. It is so big that all of Earth's land could fit inside it.

Most of the salt in salt water comes from the weathering of rocks. Rivers carry the salts from the rocks into ocean waters. Some inland seas and lakes also contain salt water.

▲ In some places fresh water is scarce. This water treatment plant removes the salt from ocean water to make fresh water.

The continents are really islands of land surrounded by Earth's large oceans. ▶

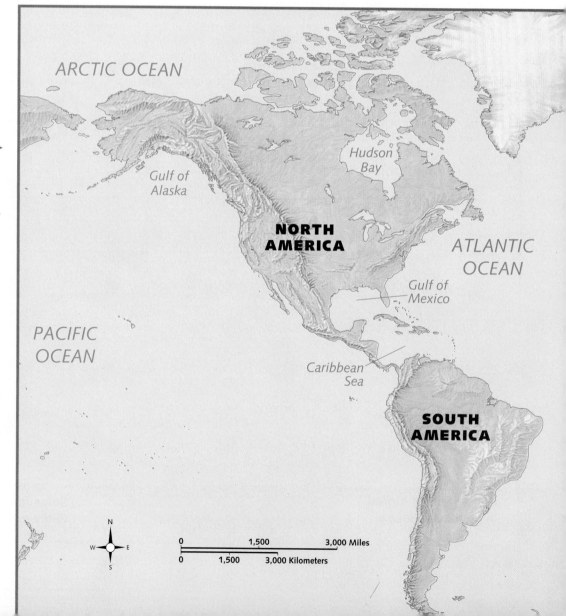

ARCTIC OCEAN

Hudson Bay

Gulf of Alaska

NORTH AMERICA

ATLANTIC OCEAN

Gulf of Mexico

PACIFIC OCEAN

Caribbean Sea

SOUTH AMERICA

N
W E
S

0   1,500   3,000 Miles

0   1,500   3,000 Kilometers

The Great Salt Lake in Utah is one of the world's saltiest bodies of water.

You may think that ocean water isn't important because you don't drink it. But ocean water helps keep the planet from being very cold in some places and very hot in others. The sun warms ocean water near the equator. This warm water moves through the ocean, warming the cooler water around it as it moves.

The warm water helps keep the air above it warm, too.

The resources of the ocean are important. Fish and other ocean animals and plants are food for millions of people. Many useful products come from the ocean. For example, people pump oil from wells deep under the ocean. About one-fourth of our oil comes from wells under the sea.

✔ **Where is salt water found on Earth?**

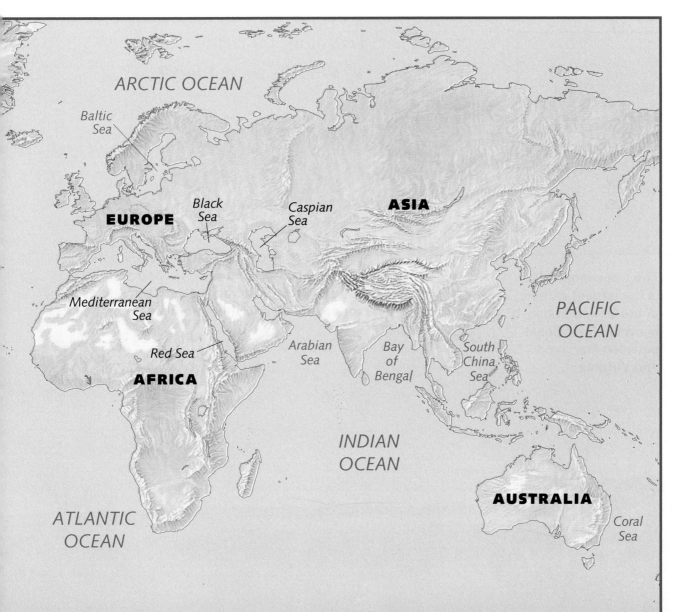

Where Fresh Water and Salt Water Meet

Suppose you could walk along the whole coast of the United States. As you walked, you would find places where rivers bring fresh water to the ocean. These places are estuaries. An **estuary** (ES•tyoo•air•ee) is a place where fresh water from a river mixes with salt water from the ocean.

Estuaries are unusual ecosystems. The plants and animals there must be able to live in both fresh water and salt water.

PENNSYLVANIA
NEW JERSEY
DELAWARE
MARYLAND
VIRGINIA
Chesapeake Bay

▲ The Chesapeake Bay is the largest estuary in the United States. It is on the East Coast between Maryland and Virginia.

Many kinds of animals live in or near estuaries. Birds build their nests in the plants on the edges of estuaries. Young fish, crabs, clams, shrimp, and oysters live and grow in the shallow waters of an estuary. Many people make their living by catching these animals, which are then sold as food.

Estuaries are important for other reasons, too. The roots of the many plants that live there slow down the water that enters the estuary. The roots also trap the soil that the slow water carries. This helps build up the land along the coast.

✔ **What is an estuary?**

Tall grasses grow around the edges of estuaries. Many birds and other animals find food and shelter there. The roots trap soil and provide a home for small fish and other animals. ▼

▲ Mangrove trees grow in estuaries that are warm all year long. Because of the way their roots grow, mangroves provide a home for small fish and other animals.

Summary

More than two-thirds of Earth's surface is covered by water. Most of this water is the salt water of oceans and seas. Fresh water is found in lakes, ponds, rivers, and streams. Nothing could live on Earth without water.

Review

1. List three ways fresh water is used.
2. How does water get underground?
3. Where do the salts in Earth's oceans come from?
4. **Critical Thinking** Why don't estuaries hold only salt water?
5. **Test Prep** Which of the following is true of all ocean water?
   A It is warm.
   B It is salt water.
   C It is fresh water.
   D It is frozen.

LINKS

MATH LINK

Graph It Use a computer graphing program such as **Graph Links** to make a bar graph that shows the part of Earth's water that is salty and the part that is fresh.

WRITING LINK

Persuasive Writing—Opinion Is it fun to visit the water? Write a paragraph describing a trip you have taken on a boat. Or describe a trip to a beach, lake, or river. What was it like? What did you do? What was the water like? Persuade others that it would be a good place to visit.

ART LINK

Mobile Find out about the kinds of animals that live in an estuary. Then make a mobile that shows some of these animals.

TECHNOLOGY LINK

Learn more about the water on Earth by visiting the National Air and Space Museum Internet Site. **www.si.edu/harcourt/science**

 Smithsonian Institution®

What Is the Water Cycle?

In this lesson, you can . . .

 INVESTIGATE how fresh water and salt water evaporate.

 LEARN ABOUT the movement of water on Earth and in the air.

 LINK to math, writing, health, and technology.

 **INVESTIGATE**

Evaporation

Activity Purpose During a storm, rain forms puddles. After the rain stops, the puddles disappear. This process is called *evaporation*. In this investigation you will **control variables** to find out if some kinds of water evaporate faster than others.

Materials

- masking tape
- 4 identical jars
- measuring cup
- water
- salt
- spoon
- 2 jar lids
- ruler

Activity Procedure

1 Put a strip of masking tape down the side of each jar. (Picture A)

2 Using the measuring cup, pour $\frac{1}{2}$ cup water into each jar. Stir a spoonful of salt into 2 of the jars. Mark these jars with an *S*. Mark the other 2 jars with an *F*.

◄ Water on these berries turned to ice in the cold night air. The sun's heat will melt the ice.

D14

3 Make a mark on the tape on each jar to show how high the water is. Then put the lids on one *S* jar and one *F* jar. (Picture B)

4 **Predict** which jar the water will evaporate from first. **Record** your prediction.

5 Place the jars in a sunny place.

6 **Observe** the jars every day for a week. Each day, mark how high the water in each jar is.

Picture A

Draw Conclusions

1. Did all the water evaporate from any of the jars? If so, which one?

2. **Compare** your prediction with your results. How did you make your prediction? Was your prediction correct?

Picture B

3. **Scientists at Work** To find the answers to some questions, scientists test things that will change. These things are called *variables*. Then they add something to the experiment that they know won't change. This is called a *control*. What were the controls in this investigation?

Investigate Further **Infer** what would happen if you repeated the activity but used different amounts of salt. How would the results change? Try the activity to see if your inference was correct. Don't forget to use controls.

Process Skill Tip

A control shows what would happen if no variable were being tested. **Controlling variables** is one way scientists make sure that their experiments are fair tests.

The Water Cycle

How Water Changes

FIND OUT

- **how water changes form**
- **how water moves from place to place**

VOCABULARY

evaporation
condensation
precipitation
water cycle

Water is the only material on Earth that has three forms in nature. You can find liquid water in lakes and rivers. You can find ice on a freezing winter day. Water is in the air around you in the form of a gas you can't see. It is called water vapor.

The form that water takes depends on the amount of heat, or *thermal energy,* in it. Adding heat or taking away heat changes the form of water.

Water changes form as temperatures change. The warm rays of the sun melt ice. Cold temperatures turn liquid water back into ice again. The sun warms a rain puddle, and the water becomes invisible water vapor.

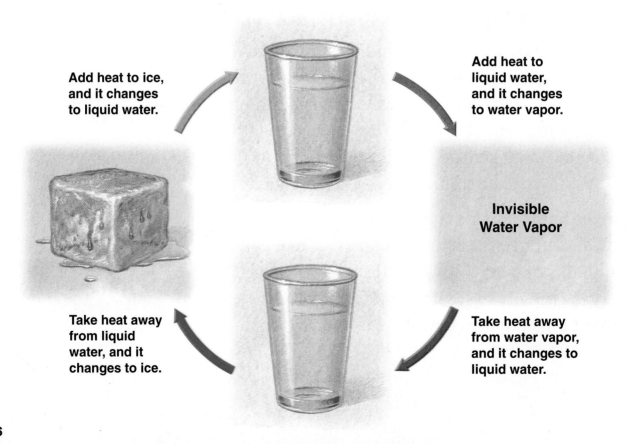

Add heat to ice, and it changes to liquid water.

Add heat to liquid water, and it changes to water vapor.

Invisible Water Vapor

Take heat away from liquid water, and it changes to ice.

Take heat away from water vapor, and it changes to liquid water.

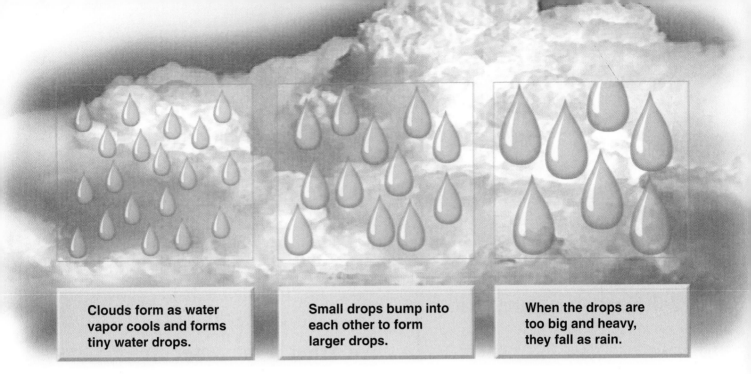

Clouds form as water vapor cools and forms tiny water drops.

Small drops bump into each other to form larger drops.

When the drops are too big and heavy, they fall as rain.

In the investigation you used the sun to heat water. The heat changed the liquid water in the open jars into a gas that spread out in the air. **Evaporation** is the changing of a liquid into a gas. Heat must be added to a liquid to make it evaporate. Evaporation changes liquid water into invisible gas—water vapor.

Water vapor in the air can condense to form dew. You can see dew on spider webs and on leaves on cool mornings. ▼

When you see rain falling, you are seeing what happens because of cooling. **Condensation** is the changing of a gas into a liquid. Taking heat away from a gas, or cooling it, changes the gas into a liquid. When water vapor cools, the water changes form. It becomes liquid water.

✔ **What three forms can water take?**

Water vapor in the air can also freeze as it condenses, to form frost. Air must be cold for frost to form. ▼

Water Changes and Moves

Water evaporates all the time from Earth's surface. So why hasn't all the water on Earth turned into water vapor? After water becomes vapor, it cools to form water again. The water returns to Earth as precipitation. **Precipitation** is water that falls to Earth as rain, snow, sleet, or hail.

Earth uses the same water over and over again. The water you use to brush your teeth is billions of years old. This recycling of water over and over again is called the water cycle. The **water cycle** is the movement of water from Earth's surface into the air and back to the surface again. This cycle is powered by heat from the sun. The picture below shows how the water cycle works.

✔ **What is the water cycle?**

The Water Cycle The sun's rays warm the land and water on Earth's surface. This causes water to evaporate and form water vapor. Warm air carries water vapor upward.

Cooler temperatures high in the air make water vapor condense. Little water droplets form clouds.

Water droplets join to make bigger drops. Rain or snow falls from clouds.

Rivers take some of the rain to oceans.

Rain flows across the ground. It goes into rivers and lakes.

Some of the rain soaks into the soil. It becomes groundwater.

The sun warms the water. Water evaporates from oceans, rivers, and lakes to start the cycle again.

Summary

Evaporation changes water from a liquid into a gas. Condensation changes water from a gas back into a liquid. The water cycle is the movement of water from Earth's surface into the air and back to the surface again. The water moves by evaporation and condensation.

Review

1. What is evaporation?
2. What is condensation?
3. What is the water cycle?
4. **Critical Thinking** What would happen if water could evaporate but could not condense?
5. **Test Prep** How does water on land return to Earth's oceans in the water cycle?

    A by evaporating
    B by turning to ice
    C by the flow of rivers
    D by entering plants

LINKS

MATH LINK

How Much Water? Suppose that 100 liters of water evaporate from a lake; 50 liters fall back on the lake as rain; 10 liters turn to ice on a mountain. The rest of the water flows back to the lake from a river. How much of the 100 liters does the river carry?

WRITING LINK

Informative Writing—Description Find pictures in magazines that show the parts of the water cycle. For each picture, write a sentence that tells what is happening. Share your work with a family member.

HEALTH LINK

Keeping Cool Evaporation helps keep your body cool on a hot day. Look up *perspiration* in a health book to find out how.

TECHNOLOGY LINK

Learn more about how people use technology to control water by watching *Inflatable Dams* on the **Harcourt Science Newsroom Video.**

CNN. Turner Le@rning

A Filter for Clean WATER

Scientists developed a filter to clean water in the space shuttle. Now they are using what they learned to clean water on Earth.

Why Clean Water?

In the United States, most people use water that has been cleaned at a water treatment plant or pumped from the ground. You get water from the faucet, knowing it is safe to drink. Some places in the world, however, don't have clean water. The people in those places often drink unsafe water. The World Health Organization estimates that one

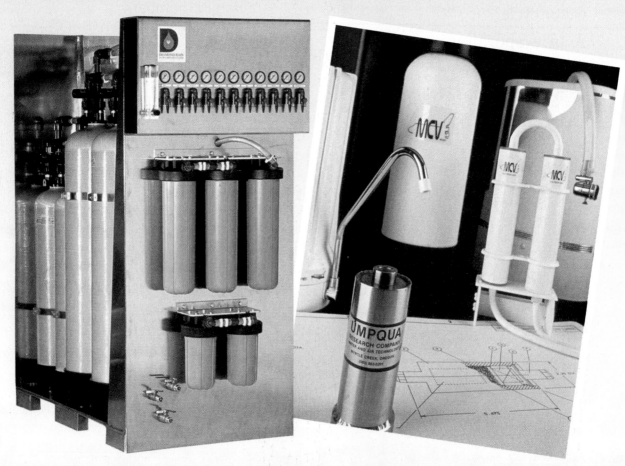

billion people are not able to get clean, safe drinking water every day.

Water in Space

Astronauts taking long space flights need lots of water. But water is heavy and takes up a lot of room. The space shuttle can't carry all the clean water that astronauts need. So scientists at NASA and at the Umpqua Research Company developed a filter to clean the used water on the space shuttle. Astronauts take only a little water on each mission, and they use the filter to clean the water after they use it.

The Umpqua Filter

After its success in space, scientists decided to use the filter on Earth. Communities suffering from natural disasters like floods and hurricanes need to clean their water. So do communities that don't already have water treatment systems.

The Umpqua filter doesn't remove dirt and chemicals from the water. It only kills bacteria. So water is first passed through another filter that removes dirt and chemicals. Then it goes through the Umpqua filter.

Several companies are now making small water-cleaning systems that use the Umpqua filter to kill bacteria in water. These filters last a long time. And it costs less than one cent per gallon to clean water by using these systems.

Think About It

1. Why is cleaning water at a disaster site better than shipping in bottled water?
2. Why is it important for people to have clean water to drink?

WEB LINK:
For Science and Technology updates, visit the Harcourt Internet site.
www.harcourtschool.com

Careers | Environmental Technician

What They Do Environmental technicians look for sources of pollution in the environment, especially in water. They also look for ways to control that pollution.

Education and Training An environmental technician needs to study environmental science and math. It is also important for a technician to learn to write and speak well.

Lisa Rossbacher
GEOLOGIST

When you think of the National Aeronautics and Space Administration (NASA), you may not think of rocks and minerals. But some people who work at NASA study rocks and minerals. Learning about rocks and landforms on Earth helps us understand more about other planets.

Lisa Rossbacher has helped NASA study erosion on the planet Mars. She uses maps and photographs taken by space probes. She compares the patterns of erosion she sees on Mars with those she has studied on Earth. From her observations she makes inferences about how the landforms on Mars may have been shaped. She has inferred that water once moved over the surface of Mars, just as it does on Earth. Other geologists agree with her.

Rossbacher applies what she learns from her studies to help people. Geologists such as Rossbacher can help people by telling them where floods, landslides,

earthquakes, or sinkholes are likely to occur. Once a community knows about the danger, it can make plans to use the land wisely. For example, people who live in areas that may flood might build dams to control the flow of water. In areas where earthquakes are likely, builders try to make buildings safer in case of an earthquake.

Think About It

1. What kinds of science skills does Rossbacher use in her work?
2. How might you use photographs of Mars to study erosion there?

Cloud in a Jar

How do raindrops form?

Materials

- metal pie pan
- freezer
- glass jar without lid
- hot water
- ice cubes

Procedure

❶ Put the pan in the freezer for an hour.

❷ Just before you take the pan out, have your teacher fill the jar half way with hot water.

❸ Remove the pan from the freezer, and fill it with ice cubes. Place the pan on top of the jar. Leave it there for a few minutes.

Draw Conclusions

Observe what happens inside the jar. How is this like part of the water cycle?

Making Raindrops

Why do raindrops fall?

Materials

- dropper
- water
- clear plastic coffee-can lid
- pencil

Procedure

❶ Fill the dropper with water.

❷ Turn the lid so the top of the lid rests flat on the table. Drop small drops of water onto the lid. Put as many drops as you can on the lid without having the drops touch.

❸ Quickly turn the lid over.

❹ Holding the lid upside down, move drops together with the pencil point. What happens?

Draw Conclusions

How is this similar to what happens in clouds?

Chapter 1 Review and Test Preparation

Vocabulary Review

Use the terms below to complete the sentences 1 through 6. The page numbers in ( ) tell you where to look in the chapter if you need help.

groundwater (D8)

estuary (D12)

evaporation (D17)

condensation (D17)

precipitation (D18)

water cycle (D18)

1. Water that falls to Earth as rain, snow, sleet, or hail is ___.

2. The process that changes a liquid into a gas is ___.

3. An ___ is a place where fresh water from a river mixes with salt water from the ocean.

4. The process that changes a gas into a liquid is ___.

5. The ___ is the movement of water from Earth's surface into the air and back to the surface again.

6. Fresh water found under Earth's surface is ___.

Connect Concepts

Write the terms where they belong in the concept map. Use the terms in the Word Bank. One term will be used twice.

water vapor   **liquid water**   **ice**

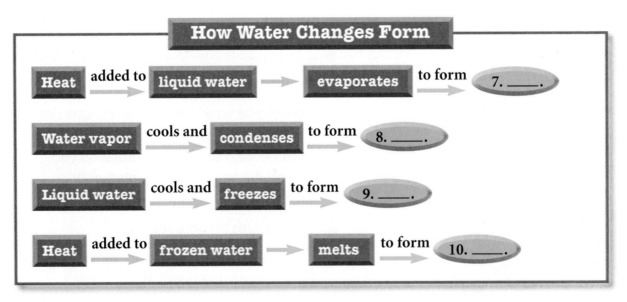

Check Understanding

Write the letter of the best choice.

11. Which is mostly water?
    A rocks   C shells
    B plants   D soil

12. The oceans help control —
    F types of soil
    G temperature
    H groundwater
    J sunlight

13. Where does the energy for the water cycle come from?
    A the sun   C the soil
    B the wind   D the ocean

14. Fresh water is **NOT** found —
    F under Earth's surface
    G in lakes
    H in oceans
    J in rivers

15. Rain and snow are forms of —
    A precipitation
    B transpiration
    C condensation
    D evaporation

Critical Thinking

16. Some people think Earth's glaciers are important resources. Why might they think so?

17. Why is it important to not pour paint, oil, and other harmful liquids down a drain?

18. Why is an estuary an important environment?

19. Explain why the sun is important to the water cycle.

Process Skills Review

20. Suppose you are asked to keep track of the water used by your class. Tell how **using numbers** could make it easier to organize this data.

21. You see drops of rain falling. How could you **make a model** to find out what happens to the rain? Tell how you could **control variables** to find out.

Performance Assessment

Diagram the Water Cycle

Work with a partner. Together, draw a simple picture of the water cycle. Label the changes in the water. Tell whether water has been warmed or cooled to make each change.

D25

Observing Weather

No matter where you go, it seems someone is talking about the weather. That's because the weather affects what people do every day. Should you wear a coat? Will it rain during your picnic? Many of life's decisions depend on the weather.

Vocabulary Preview

atmosphere
weather
temperature
front
wind
anemometer
weather map

⫸FAST FACT

Called the "snow eater," the Chinook is a hot wind that roars down the Rocky Mountains in winter. Within seconds, a Chinook can go from a gentle breeze to over 160 kilometers (100 mi) per hour, melting several feet of snow in just a few hours!

The biggest storms on Earth are hurricanes. If the energy in one average hurricane could be captured, it would supply the United States with electricity for six months!

Record Hurricanes

Record Type	Where	When	Name
Deadliest 6000 killed	Galveston, Texas	1900	unnamed
Strongest 322 kph (200 mph) winds	Florida Keys	1935	"Labor Day"
Costliest $25 billion	Louisiana and South Florida	1992	Andrew

What Is Weather?

In this lesson, you can . . .

INVESTIGATE
the properties of air.

LEARN ABOUT
what weather is.

LINK to math, writing, social studies, and technology.

INVESTIGATE

Properties of Air

Activity Purpose Air is all around you. You can't see it, but you can **observe** its properties. In this investigation you will make observations. Then you will use them to **infer** some of the properties of air.

Materials

- plastic container
- water
- paper towel
- plastic cup
- index card

Activity Procedure

Part A

1 Half-fill the plastic container with water.

2 Crumple the paper towel. Push it to the bottom of the plastic cup.

◀ Water in the air can form clouds. These tall storm clouds are called thunderheads.

3 Turn the cup upside down. Push the cup to the bottom of the plastic container. Do not tilt the cup as you are pushing it downward. Then pull the cup straight up and out of the water. **Observe** the paper towel. **Record** your observations. (Picture A)

Part B

4 Remove the paper towel from the cup. Half-fill the cup with water. Put the index card over the cup opening.

Picture A

5 Hold the cup over the plastic container. Use your right hand to hold the cup and your left hand to hold the index card in place. Quickly turn the cup over. Take your left hand off the index card. **Record** your observations. (Picture B)

Draw Conclusions

1. What did you **observe** in Part A?

2. What did you **observe** in Part B?

3. **Scientists at Work** Scientists **observe** things that happen all around them. They use their observations to **infer** why those things happen. Use your observations to infer one property of air for each part of this investigation.

Picture B

Investigate Further Suppose you repeat Part B with a cup that is almost filled with water. **Predict** what will happen. Then try it.

Process Skill Tip

When you **observe**, you use your senses to examine things. Then you can **record** what you observe. When you **infer**, you use your observations to explain why something happens.

Where Weather Happens

FIND OUT

- about the layers of the atmosphere
- what weather is

VOCABULARY

atmosphere
weather

The Air Around You

It's easy to observe the air around you. But how do you study the air high above the planet? Long before the airplane was invented, scientists had wanted to study air high above the Earth. Some scientists put weather instruments on kites that they sent into the atmosphere. The **atmosphere** (AT•muhs•feer) is the air that surrounds Earth.

Today we know a lot about the atmosphere. We know that it has layers. We also know that the air in the atmosphere has certain properties. Air takes up space. That's why the paper towel in the cup stayed dry. Air also has weight and presses on things. In the investigation air pushed up on the index card, holding it in place. This pressing by the air is called *air pressure.*

The atmosphere acts like a blanket for Earth. The sun shines on Earth's surface and warms it. The surface gives off heat. Earth's atmosphere holds in the heat. Without the atmosphere, most of the energy that keeps Earth warm would escape into space.

✓ **What is the atmosphere?**

◄ A person flew in a hot-air balloon for the first time in 1783. After that, scientists flew in balloons to study the atmosphere.

The Atmosphere

The atmosphere has layers. You can't see where the layers begin and end. But the air in each layer is different.

1 thermosphere

2 mesosphere

3 stratosphere

4 troposphere

1 Temperatures in the *thermosphere* (THER·muhs·feer) can be higher than 2,000°C (3,632°F). Air particles can be miles apart in this part of the atmosphere. Some parts of this layer glow as the sun's rays hit them. Those parts form the northern and southern lights.

2 Temperatures are lower in the *mesosphere* (MES·uhs·feer) and can go below ⁻120°C (⁻184°F).

3 The *stratosphere* (STRAT·uhs·feer) contains the atmosphere's ozone. Ozone is a type of oxygen. It absorbs harmful rays from the sun. Because ozone absorbs some of the sun's energy, temperatures increase as you go higher in the stratosphere. Even so, the temperatures are usually below freezing. Long-distance jets sometimes fly low in the stratosphere.

4 The *troposphere* (TROH·puhs·feer) is the layer of the atmosphere where you live. Air particles in this layer are close enough for you to breathe easily. All our weather takes place in the troposphere. Near the surface, temperatures are warm. But the higher you go in the troposphere, the cooler the air temperature gets. At the top of the troposphere, the temperature drops to ⁻80°C (⁻112°F).

Weather

Earth's atmosphere is more than 160 kilometers (100 mi) thick. But weather takes place only in the 10 kilometers (6 mi) of air directly above Earth's surface.

Everybody talks about the weather, but what is it? **Weather** is what is happening in the atmosphere at a certain place. Temperature, wind, and precipitation are all parts of weather. There would be no weather without the sun. The sun's heat causes clouds, winds, and precipitation to form.

Meteorologists are scientists who study weather and the atmosphere. They measure and record changes in air. These changes help them know if the weather will be sunny or stormy.

✔ **What is weather?**

▲ Blizzards are large snowstorms. They have low temperatures and strong winds of 50 kilometers per hour (about 31 mph) or more. These winds blow the snow so that it is almost impossible to see.

▲ Hurricanes are strong, dangerous storms that form over warm ocean waters. Hurricanes have winds of 120 kilometers per hour (about 75 mph) or more.

Rain can come as gentle showers or pouring storms. ▼

▲ Tornadoes are violent windstorms. The winds are so strong that they can destroy homes and lift trains from their tracks. More tornadoes occur in the United States than anywhere else on Earth.

Summary

The atmosphere has layers. Weather takes place in the lowest layer of the atmosphere. Weather is what is happening in the atmosphere at a certain place. Temperature, wind, and precipitation are all parts of weather.

Review

1. List three properties of air.
2. What does ozone do?
3. List three things that are parts of the weather.
4. **Critical Thinking** What might Earth be like without the atmosphere?
5. **Test Prep** Where does weather happen?
   - **A** in the layer of the atmosphere next to Earth's surface
   - **B** in the coldest layer of the atmosphere
   - **C** where air particles are far apart
   - **D** in the ozone layer

LINKS

MATH LINK

Wind Speed How windy has it been lately? Look on the weather page in a newspaper to find out. Record the wind speed for seven days. Write the speeds in order from most windy to least windy.

WRITING LINK

Expressive Writing—Poem
Pick a type of weather, and write the letters of the name down the side of a page. For each letter, think of words that describe the weather. Use your words to make a poem for a younger child.

SOCIAL STUDIES LINK

Bad Weather Report on the worst weather disaster that has happened where you live. Interview someone who was there. Record the interview on tape, and share it with others.

TECHNOLOGY LINK

Learn more about weather by visiting the National Air and Space Museum Internet Site.
www.si.edu/harcourt/science

 Smithsonian Institution®

D33

INVESTIGATE

LESSON 2

How Are Weather Conditions Measured?

In this lesson, you can . . .

 INVESTIGATE how a thermometer works.

 LEARN ABOUT how weather is measured.

 LINK to math, writing, physical education, and technology.

Measuring Temperature

Activity Purpose Temperatures change from place to place. In this investigation you will **use numbers** and a simple thermometer to **compare** temperatures.

Materials

- water
- 1-L plastic bottle
- red food coloring
- clear drinking straw
- clay
- clear plastic cup
- dropper
- metric ruler

Activity Procedure

1 Put water in the bottle until it is almost full. Add ten drops of food coloring.

2 Put the straw in the bottle. Three-fourths of the straw should stick out of the bottle. Seal the opening around the straw with clay. (Picture A)

◄ **Weather vanes show wind direction. The head of the lobster points toward the direction the wind is blowing.**

3 Half-fill the cup with water. Add three drops of food coloring.

4 Use the dropper to put water from the cup into the straw. Add water until you can see the water in the straw above the clay stopper.

Picture A **Picture B**

5 Make a mark at the water level in the straw. You have made a thermometer. The higher the level of liquid in the straw, the higher the temperature.

6 Take the thermometer to five different places at school. Leave it at each place for 15 minutes. Use a ruler to **measure** the water level in the straw from the mark to the top of the water level. Do not squeeze the bottle while you measure. **Record** the measurement and the location. (Picture B)

Draw Conclusions

1. What happened to the water levels in the straw in the different locations?

2. What information could you learn by using your thermometer? What information is impossible to learn by using your thermometer?

3. **Scientists at Work** Scientists sometimes **use numbers** to put things in order. Look at the numbers you recorded. Use the numbers to order the locations from warmest to coolest.

Process Skill Tip

You can **use numbers** to do many things. You can count, put things in order, and **compare** one set of things to another.

How Weather Is Measured

FIND OUT

- **how weather changes**
- **the ways temperature, precipitation, and wind are measured**

VOCABULARY

temperature
front
wind
anemometer

Measuring Temperature

The highest temperature ever measured on Earth was 58°C (136°F) in northern Africa. The lowest temperature was ⁻89°C (⁻128°F) in Antarctica. **Temperature** is a measure of how hot or cold something is. Temperatures on Earth can feel burning hot or freezing cold. Thermometers are used to measure temperatures.

Air temperature is always changing. You've probably noticed changes in temperature from day to night. Air is warmer in the sun. It is cooler after the sun sets. During the day the sun warms the ground more in some places than in others. It warms land faster than water.

Temperature	
40°C/104°F	Heat wave
30°C/86°F	Good day for a swim
20°C/68°F	Perfect day!
10°C/50°F	A bit chilly—wear a light jacket!
0°C/32°F	Time for a coat (water freezes)
⁻10°C/14°F	Bundle up! It's cold outside!
⁻20°C/⁻4°F	There's ice on the windows!
⁻40°C/⁻40°F	Brrrrrr! Stay inside!

Usually, air over land is warm and dry. Air over water is cool and damp. A large body of air with the same temperature and moisture is called an *air mass.* An air mass can be hundreds of kilometers wide. It can cover many states or a whole ocean. A moving air mass causes many weather changes.

✔ **What is temperature?**

Air masses are always moving. A front is a place where two air masses of different temperatures meet. Most weather changes happen at fronts.

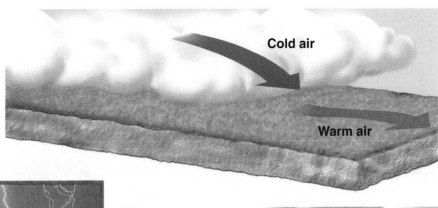

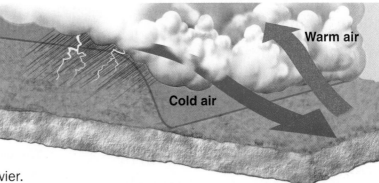

At a cold front, cold air bumps into warmer air. The cold air is heavier. It pushes the warm air up quickly. This forms tall clouds and thunderstorms. Wind and heavy rain often occur. Cold fronts move fast, so the rain doesn't last long. Cold air replaces the warm air at the surface. This makes the temperature drop after the rain.

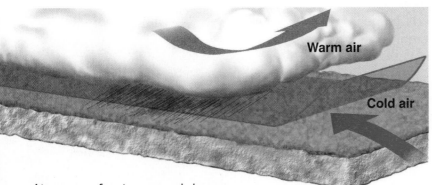

At a warm front, warm air bumps into colder air. The warm air is pushed up gently by the cold air. It forms a long line of clouds. Warm fronts bring long periods of gentle rain, gray skies, and light winds. Warm air replaces the cold air at the surface. This makes the temperature rise after the rain.

Measuring Precipitation

Many people live near rivers. Rivers are usually good neighbors, helping people move goods, supplying sources of power, and providing places to fish and swim. But when there are heavy rains, rivers can rise and spill over their banks. Flood waters can cover fields and towns, causing much damage.

People need to know when a flood might occur. That's why it's important to measure precipitation. Precipitation is any kind of water that falls from the sky. It might be rain, snow, sleet, or hail.

Meteorologists measure rain by using rain gauges. A rain gauge looks like a cup or a glass. It collects precipitation as it falls.

Meteorologists measure snow by using snow boards. Snow boards are like long rulers. People stick them into snow to see how high it is. During storms, people measure snow levels every six hours. It takes 10 inches of snow to equal the amount of water in 1 inch of rain.

✔ **How is precipitation measured?**

Rain gauges, like this one, are used to measure precipitation. ▶

The ways clouds look often give us clues about the coming weather. Stratus clouds are low gray clouds. They usually show that rain is on the way. ▼

Cumulus clouds are puffy and white. Small cumulus clouds appear in clear, sunny weather. If the clouds gather and grow tall, a storm is coming. ▼

Inside a Thunderhead

Thunderheads are giant clouds that form along cold fronts.

Strong upward movement of air causes tall clouds to form.

Quickly rising air

Sinking air

As the clouds grow taller, the air inside them cools and begins to sink.

Lightning

Strong winds

Heavy rainfall

Heavy rains, lightning, and sometimes hail and tornadoes form as air moves up and down within the cloud.

Eventually, the air cools so much that it is no longer pushed upward. Then the rain stops, and the cloud breaks up.

Measuring Wind

Winds can be helpful. They cool us on a hot day. They clear pollution from the air. But winds also can do damage. They can blow down buildings or tear up trees.

Wind is the movement of air. Wind happens because air pressure is different in different places. Air, in the form of wind, moves from areas of high pressure to areas of low pressure—like water flowing downhill.

The direction the wind comes from can be recorded, and its speed can be measured. A weather vane shows wind direction. An **anemometer** (an•uh•MAHM•uht•er) measures wind speed.

Beaufort Wind Scale

One way to estimate the speed of the wind is to look at the movements of objects around you. The pictures show one way to estimate the speed of the wind. This wind scale is called the Beaufort (BO•furt) Wind Scale.

0 Air is still; smoke rises straight up.

1 Smoke drifts; flags hang still.

2 Smoke drifts with wind.

3 Flags and leaves move gently.

4 Loose paper blows.

5 Small waves on water.

6 Umbrellas blow inside out.

7 Hard to walk into wind.

8 Branches ripped off trees.

9 Roofs and chimneys damaged.

10 Trees snapped in half.

11 Cars turned over.

12 Buildings destroyed.

The strongest winds occur in storms. Hurricanes are the biggest storms on Earth. They can be 650 kilometers (400 mi) across. The slowest hurricane winds are 120 kilometers per hour (75 mph).

Tornadoes are shaped like spinning funnels. They are much smaller than hurricanes, but they have stronger winds. The wind at the center of a tornado can be more than 480 kilometers per hour (300 mph).

✔ **What is wind?**

Summary

Many weather changes happen at fronts. People use tools to measure changes in weather. Thermometers measure temperature. Rain gauges measure rainfall. Anemometers measure wind speed.

Review

1. What is an air mass?
2. What is a front?
3. What makes the wind blow?
4. **Critical Thinking** What changes happen when a front passes through an area?
5. **Test Prep** An anemometer measures wind —
   A direction   C sounds
   B destruction   D speed

LINKS

MATH LINK

Temperature Table Make a table showing each day's high and low temperature for 1 week. Which day had the greatest difference in temperature? What was the difference?

WRITING LINK

Informative Writing— Description Write a paragraph to describe today's weather. How does the weather make you feel? Read your description in class. Compare your description with those of your classmates.

PHYSICAL EDUCATION LINK

Fly a Kite Find directions for making a kite. Look in books with projects on wind, weather, air, and Earth science. Fly your kite on different days when the wind is blowing at different speeds. When does your kite fly best?

TECHNOLOGY LINK

To learn more about measuring weather, watch *Phoenix Monsoon* on the **Harcourt Science Newsroom Video.**

What Is a Weather Map?

In this lesson, you can . . .

 INVESTIGATE how to read a weather map.

 LEARN ABOUT the way people predict weather.

 LINK to math, writing, social studies, and technology.

 **INVESTIGATE**

Reading Weather Maps

Activity Purpose Maps show a lot of data. Often the data is shown as symbols. In this investigation you will **interpret data** on a weather map. Then you will answer questions about the weather.

Materials
- weather map

Activity Procedure

1 Study the weather map and the key to the symbols that it uses.

2 Use the map to answer the questions.

◀ These red and black flags tell people that a hurricane is coming.

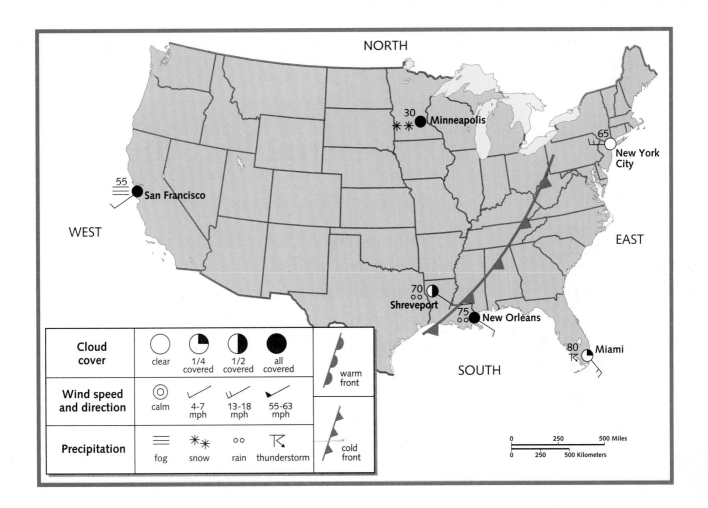

Draw Conclusions

1. Where is there a thunderstorm?

2. Find the cold front. What can you tell about the weather along the cold front?

3. **Scientists at Work** Scientists **interpret data** on weather maps to learn about the weather in different places. Interpret data on this map to describe the weather in Minneapolis, Minnesota.

Investigate Further The weather in the United States generally moves from west to east. Imagine that you are in New York City. Use the data on the map to **predict** what your weather may be like about one week from now.

Forecasting Weather

FIND OUT

- how people forecast the weather

- how to read a weather map

VOCABULARY

weather map

Gathering Weather Data

You turn on the TV. Joyce Bishop, the weather forecaster, stands in front of a big map. She points to it and says there will be rain tomorrow. So you know you should take an umbrella to school.

You depend on the TV weather forecaster. But she doesn't predict the weather by herself. She has help.

Information about the weather comes from thousands of weather stations all over the world. At each station, data about temperature, precipitation, air pressure, wind, and clouds are recorded.

◄ Thousands of stations collect weather data each day. The government runs some of the stations like this one. Some people have instruments at their homes to collect data.

▲ Weather satellites circle Earth many times each day. Satellite data can show cloud patterns over large areas.

D44

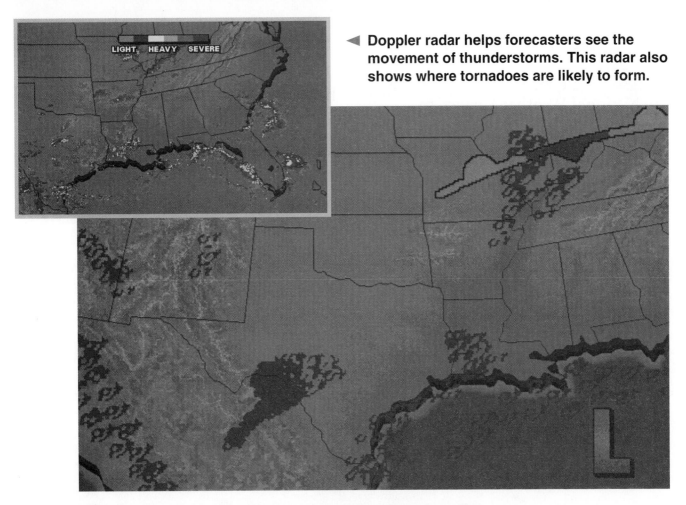

◄ Doppler radar helps forecasters see the movement of thunderstorms. This radar also shows where tornadoes are likely to form.

LIGHT HEAVY SEVERE

▲ TV weather forecasters get data and forecasts from the National Weather Service. Sometimes they use the data to make their own forecasts for a local area.

Weather planes gather data about storms. Meteorologists on these planes try to find out how strong the winds are and what direction a storm is likely to move.

Data also comes from weather balloons. Meteorologists send up weather balloons every 12 hours. Instruments carried by the balloons take readings of temperature, precipitation, and wind. They record data on weather high in the atmosphere.

Satellites in space send weather data back to Earth. Satellites also take pictures that show clouds and storms as they move across the country.

Each day the National Weather Service collects all these pieces of data. The data goes into computers that organize the information into maps. Computers also help meteorologists make predictions. They send all this information to the weather forecasters you see on TV.

✔ **Name three sources of weather data.**

Weather Maps

Meteorologists use the data from the National Weather Service to make forecasts. They also use the data to make weather maps. A **weather map** is a map that shows weather data for a large area. The maps show temperatures and precipitation. They show warm fronts and cold fronts. They show areas of high air pressure and low air pressure.

Some weather maps use station-model symbols. You saw some of these symbols in the investigation. A station model is shown on the next page. Meteorologists often use these symbols instead of the symbols used in many newspapers. These symbols give more exact data about the weather in a certain place.

✔ **What is a weather map?**

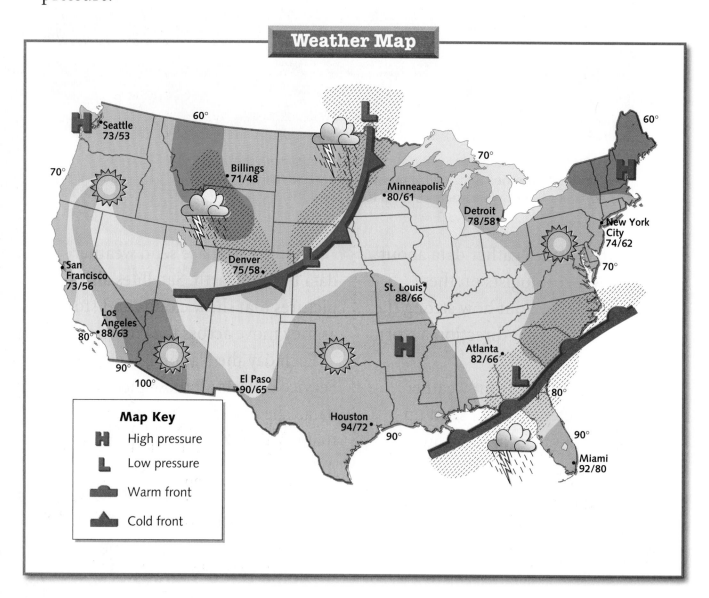

Weather Map

Seattle 73/53

60°

70°

Billings 71/48

60°

70°

Minneapolis 80/61

Detroit 78/58

New York City 74/62

70°

San Francisco 73/56

Denver 75/58

St. Louis 88/66

Los Angeles 88/63

80°

El Paso 90/65

Atlanta 82/66

90°

100°

Houston 94/72

80°

90°

Miami 92/80

Map Key

H High pressure

L Low pressure

  Warm front

  Cold front

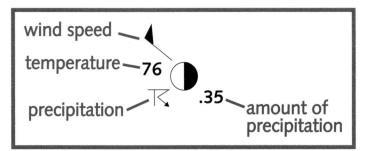

wind speed

temperature — 76

precipitation

.35 — amount of precipitation

▲ A station model shows the weather at one place. The weather at this station is cloudy with winds out of the northwest at about 55–63 miles per hour. The temperature is 76°F, and there are thunderstorms.

Summary

Meteorologists use data from surface stations, airplanes, weather balloons, and satellites. Weather maps use symbols to show weather conditions over large areas.

Review

1. What kinds of weather data do we get from airplanes?
2. How do satellites help meteorologists predict the weather?
3. What is a station model?
4. **Critical Thinking** Why do meteorologists collect data many times each day?
5. **Test Prep** A weather map does **NOT** show —
   A temperature
   B precipitation
   C seasons
   D wind speed

LINKS

MATH LINK

Forecast Fractions Keep track of the TV weather forecast for five days. Each day check to see if the forecast was right or wrong. Write a fraction to compare how many forecasts were right (top number) with the total number of forecasts (bottom number).

WRITING LINK

Informative Writing— Explanation Suppose a meteorologist comes to your class. Write one question about weather. With your classmates, find the answers to the questions. Publish your findings.

SOCIAL STUDIES LINK

Types of Maps A weather map is only one kind of map. Find another kind of map in a book or a magazine. Explain to the class what the map shows.

TECHNOLOGY LINK

Learn more about weather maps by visiting this Internet Site.

www.scilinks.org/harcourt

Controlling Lightning Strikes

The clouds are black. The sky is dark. You know there's going to be a thunderstorm. Then you see the lightning. It flashes down from the sky in giant forks. You know you will be safe if you stay inside a building or a car. But what about all the power lines and other structures that attract lightning? How safe are they?

Lightning Damage

Each year $138 million worth of damage is caused by lightning strikes in the United States. These strikes are especially harmful to energy plants, airports, and military bases. When lightning struck an energy company in Japan, the company was unable to provide power for a week. That's hard on families, but it's even worse for hospitals and fire departments. Researchers around the world have been studying lightning, hoping to find a better way to protect buildings.

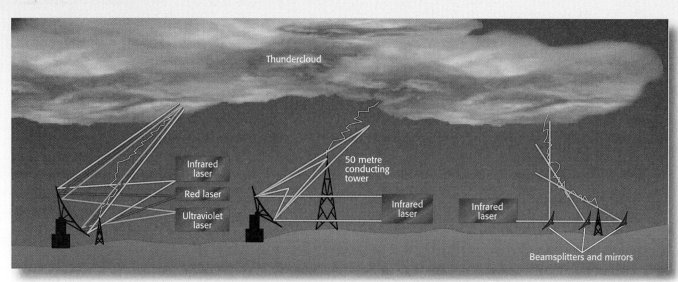

Thundercloud

Infrared laser

Red laser

Ultraviolet laser

50 metre conducting tower

Infrared laser

Infrared laser

Beamsplitters and mirrors

▲ **Some plans for attracting lightning**

Lightning Rods

The idea of protecting people and property from lightning is not new. The original idea of lightning rods began with Benjamin Franklin in 1752. A lightning rod is a metal rod that is placed on top of the highest point on a building. Because the lightning rod is the highest thing around, lightning will strike it instead of the building. When lightning strikes the rod, the electricity passes through the rod, along a cable, and harmlessly into the ground.

Using Lasers to Attract Lightning

Lightning rods wait to be hit by lightning. Now scientists are working out a way to use lasers to pull lightning out of the sky and conduct it into the ground. That way they can make lightning strike where and when they want.

Researchers began experimenting with lasers and lightning in the early 1990s. They fire ultraviolet (UV) lasers into the sky. The laser beams make a path through the air. Lightning bolts follow this path back to the laser like water flowing through a pipe. A metal plate in front of the laser protects it from the lightning. As lightning follows the laser beam, its power is turned aside harmlessly. If all goes as planned, portable lasers could be used to draw lightning away from power lines, airplanes, and important buildings.

Think About It

- Why would it be useful for lightning lasers to be portable?

WEB LINK:
For Science and Technology updates, visit the Harcourt Internet site.
www.harcourtschool.com

Careers — Weather Researcher

What They Do Weather researchers are people who work behind the scenes of the weather reports you watch on TV. Some researchers record the weather where they live. Others collect data to make charts and maps for weather prediction.

Education and Training A weather researcher needs a college degree in meteorology, math, or physics. Weather researchers also need writing skills because they often publish the results of their work.

June Bacon-Bercey

METEOROLOGIST

"I was discouraged [from becoming a meteorologist] and other women were discouraged. If they feel they've got some money behind them, it might be better."

The words above explain why June Bacon-Bercey decided to set up a scholarship fund for women who want to be meteorologists. Meteorologists are people who study weather. They observe weather and map weather conditions. They use information from computers to predict the weather.

Bacon-Bercey has been interested in the weather since she was a young girl. She has worked on television as a meteorologist. She has also worked for the National Weather Service. In 1979 she became chief administrator of

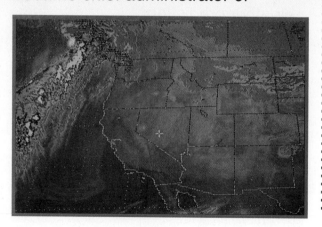

television activities for the National Oceanic and Atmospheric Administration. She coordinates the agency's services to schools, the government, and the general public.

Bacon-Bercey has seen a lot of changes in the ways weather data is gathered and shared with people. Years ago people who gave TV weather reports just read information a weather service gave them. Now many TV stations hire their own meteorologists.

Think About It

1. What might a person who studies the weather talk about if he or she came to your school?
2. If you were setting up a scholarship fund, what groups of people would you most like to help?

Measure Precipitation

How can you find out how much rain falls?

Materials

- masking tape
- ruler
- clear plastic 1-L bottle with top cut off

Procedure

1. Tape the ruler to the outside of the bottle. The 1-in. mark should be at the bottom of the bottle.

2. Put your rain gauge outside before it rains. Do not place it under a tree or under an object that might block the rain.

3. Check the amount of water in the bottle after the rain stops.

Draw Conclusions

Look on the weather page of the newspaper. How much rain fell the day you used your gauge? Was your measurement correct? How close was your measurement?

Measure the Wind

How fast does the wind blow?

Materials

- 2 cardboard strips
- stapler
- cap of a ballpoint pen
- 4 small paper cups (3 white, 1 red)
- watch with second hand
- scissors
- wire

Procedure

1. Make an X with the cardboard strips. Staple the strips together.

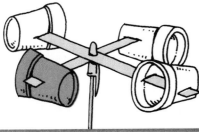

2. Use the scissors to make a hole in the middle of the X. Push the pen cap into the hole as shown

3. Cut a slit in the opposite sides of each cup. Attach the cups as shown.

4. Push the piece of wire deep into the ground outside. Balance the pen cap on the wire.

5. Count the times the red cup spins by in 1 minute. Divide this number by 10. The answer tells how many miles per hour the wind is blowing.

Draw Conclusions

Measure the speed of the wind over the next several days. How does the speed change?

Chapter 2 Review and Test Preparation

Vocabulary Review

Use the terms below to complete the sentences 1 through 8. The page numbers in ( ) tell you where to look in the chapter if you need help.

atmosphere (D30)

weather (D32)

temperature (D36)

front (D37)

wind (D40)

anemometer (D40)

weather map (D46)

1. What is happening in the atmosphere at a certain place is ___.

2. A tool that measures wind speed is an ___.

3. A ___ shows the weather over a large area.

4. The air that surrounds Earth is the ___.

5. The ___ is the measure of how hot or cold something is.

6. The movement of air is ___.

7. A ___ is a place where two air masses meet.

8. Weather occurs in the lowest layer of the ___.

Connect Concepts

Write the terms where they belong in the concept map.

anemometer   temperature

precipitation   wind vane

rain gauge

Weather Measuring Tools	
Weather Condition	**Tools That Measure It**
9. _____	thermometer
wind	11. _____
	12. _____
10. _____	13. _____
	snow board

Check Understanding

Write the letter of the best choice.

14. The atmosphere is important to our weather because —
    A it is clear
    B it holds in Earth's heat
    C winds are light
    D it has ten layers

15. At a cold front, —
    F warm air replaces cold air
    G there is gentle rain
    H winds are light
    J there can be thunderstorms

16. A ___ collects weather data on the ground.
    A satellite   C weather station
    B airplane   D weather balloon

Critical Thinking

Use the diagram below to answer the questions.

17. What type of front is shown?

18. What will the weather be like along the front?

19. How will the weather change as the front moves on?

Process Skills Review

20. **Observe** the table below, which shows the high temperature in one place for five days in a row. **Interpret the data**. What can you **infer** about the weather during the week?

Day	High Temperature (°F)
Monday	20°
Tuesday	19°
Wednesday	21°
Thursday	45°
Friday	47°

21. How would you **use numbers** to find out how much rain is equal to 10 in. of snow?

Performance Assessment

Reading Weather Maps

Use the weather map to tell what the weather is like in Charlotte, North Carolina. Next, use the data from the map to forecast how Charlotte's weather will change. Then, draw a new station model for Charlotte showing what the weather will be like after the change.

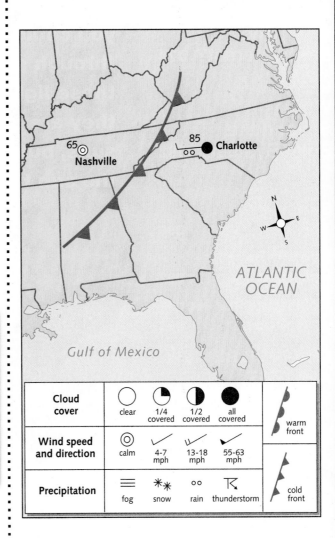

Earth and Its Place in the Solar System

Looking up at a clear night sky, you will see tiny points of light. If you could leave Earth and travel through space to get closer to those lights, you would see that they are other worlds and other suns, but not like the Earth and the sun that we know.

Vocabulary Preview

solar system	revolution
orbit	phases
planet	lunar eclipse
asteroid	solar eclipse
comet	star
rotation	constellation
axis	telescope

FAST FACT

If you want to find the coldest place in the solar system, go to Triton, Neptune's largest moon. Temperatures there average ⁻235 degrees C. It's so cold on Triton that volcanoes erupt with ice instead of lava!

The sun is big enough to hold over 1 million Earths. Even so, the sun is an average-sized star! Here's how the sun compares with some of the biggest stars that you can see in the night sky.

Star Sizes

Star	Miles Across
Sun	870,000
Mu Cephi	2,000,000,000
VV Cephi	2,000,000,000
Epsilon Auriga	46,000,000,000

This drawing shows how scientists think the surface of Triton looks.

LESSON **1**

What Is the Solar System?

In this lesson, you can . . .

 INVESTIGATE the planets.

 LEARN ABOUT objects in the solar system.

 LINK to math, writing, health, and technology.

The Planets

Activity Purpose
Nine planets circle the sun. They are not all alike. In this investigation you will use some of the planets' properties to **order** them. Then you will **classify** the planets by using the data you have organized.

Materials
- pencil
- paper

Activity Procedure

1. Copy the Ordering Planet Data chart.

2. **Use numbers** from the data table to find each planet's distance from the sun. **Record** in your table the names of the planets, beginning with the one closest to the sun.

3. **Use numbers** from the data table to find the distance across each planet. The planet with the shortest distance across is the smallest planet. Use numbers to **order** the planets by size. **Record** the names of the planets in order, beginning with the smallest planet.

◀ Telescopes help us see things that are far away.

Ordering Planet Data

Closest to the Sun to Farthest from the Sun	Smallest to Largest	Shortest Year to Longest Year

Planet Data

Planet	Distance from Sun (in millions of kilometers)	Distance Across (in kilometers)	Length of Year (y=Earth year d=Earth day)
Earth	150	✓ 12,750	365 d
Jupiter	778	✓ 143,000	12 y
Mars	228	6,800	2 y
Mercury	58	4,900	88 d
Neptune	4,505	✓ 49,000	165 y
Pluto	5,890	2,300	248 y
Saturn	1,427	✓ 120,000	29 y
Uranus	2,869	✓ 51,000	84 y
Venus	108	✓ 12,000	225 d

Draw Conclusions

1. Which planet is closest to the sun? Farthest from the sun?

2. Which is the largest planet? The smallest?

3. **Scientists at Work** Scientists sometimes **use numbers** to put things in **order**. Scientists have studied the same data you used in this investigation. How did using numbers help you realize the **space relationships** between the planets?

Process Skill Tip

You can **use numbers to order** objects. Putting objects in order allows you to **use space relationships** to describe the positions of objects.

The Solar System

FIND OUT

- the names of the planets
- about other bodies in the solar system

VOCABULARY

solar system
orbit
planet
asteroid
comet

The Structure of the Solar System

The **solar system** is the sun and the objects that orbit around it. An **orbit** is the path an object takes as it moves around another object in space. All the planets you studied in the investigation, including Earth, orbit the sun.

You learned about some parts of the solar system in the investigation. The solar system has nine planets, including Earth. A **planet** is a large body of rock or gas that orbits the sun. The solar system also has many moons. Moons are large, rocky objects that orbit planets. Earth has one moon. Other planets have no moons or many moons. Comets and asteroids are also parts of the solar system.

✔ **What is the solar system?**

THE INSIDE STORY

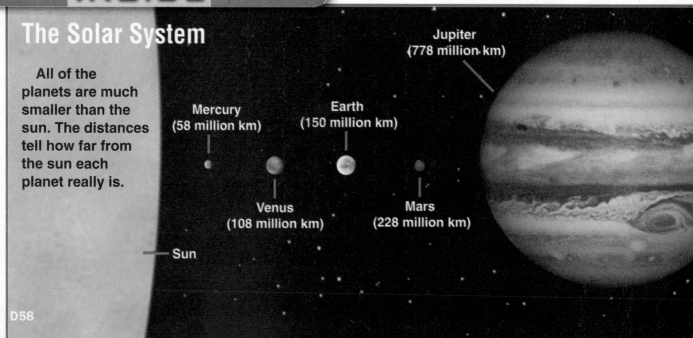

The Solar System

All of the planets are much smaller than the sun. The distances tell how far from the sun each planet really is.

Jupiter
(778 million km)

Mercury
(58 million km)

Earth
(150 million km)

Venus
(108 million km)

Mars
(228 million km)

Sun

The Sun

The sun is the center of the solar system. It is a *star*—a hot ball of glowing gases. It looks different to us from other stars because it is closer to us than other stars are.

The sun is very hot and bright. The sun is also big. All of the planets and moons of the solar system could fit inside it.

Gravity on the sun is very strong. That's because of its great size. *Gravity* is the force of one object's pull on another. The sun's gravity helps hold the objects in the solar system in orbit.

✔ **What is the sun?**

The sun is 1.35 million kilometers (about 838,900 mi) across. The Earth is tiny compared with the sun. The sun could hold more than one million Earths inside it. ▶

Saturn
(1,427 million km)

Pluto
(5,890 million km)

Uranus
(2,869 million km)

Neptune
(4,505 million km)

D59

The Inner Planets

In the investigation you found a way to put the planets in order by their distances from the sun. Scientists use this same order to put the planets into two groups. The four planets closest to the sun are in one group. They are called the *inner planets*. The five other planets are the *outer planets*.

The inner planets are Mercury, Venus, Earth, and Mars. They are alike in many ways. They all have rocky surfaces. Because they are

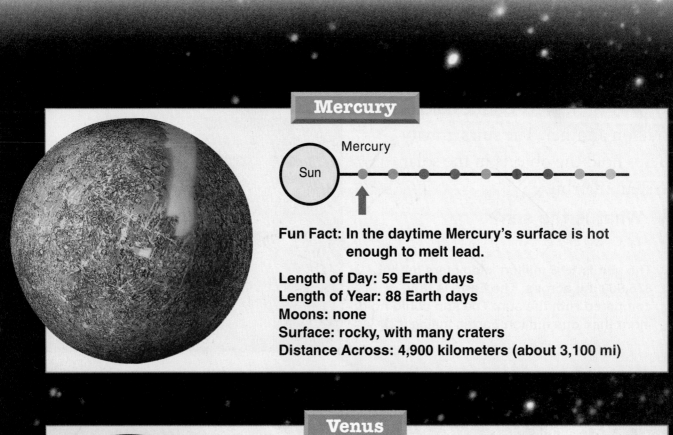

Mercury

Fun Fact: In the daytime Mercury's surface is hot enough to melt lead.

Length of Day: 59 Earth days
Length of Year: 88 Earth days
Moons: none
Surface: rocky, with many craters
Distance Across: 4,900 kilometers (about 3,100 mi)

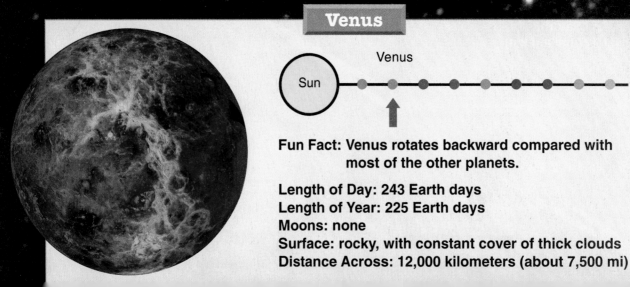

Venus

Fun Fact: Venus rotates backward compared with most of the other planets.

Length of Day: 243 Earth days
Length of Year: 225 Earth days
Moons: none
Surface: rocky, with constant cover of thick clouds
Distance Across: 12,000 kilometers (about 7,500 mi)

closer to the sun, they are warmer than the outer planets. The inner planets are also smaller than most of the outer planets. None of them has more than two moons.

Earth is different from the other inner planets. It has a watery surface. It is the only planet with a lot of oxygen in its atmosphere. Earth also has plant life and animal life.

✔ **List the inner planets in order from the sun.**

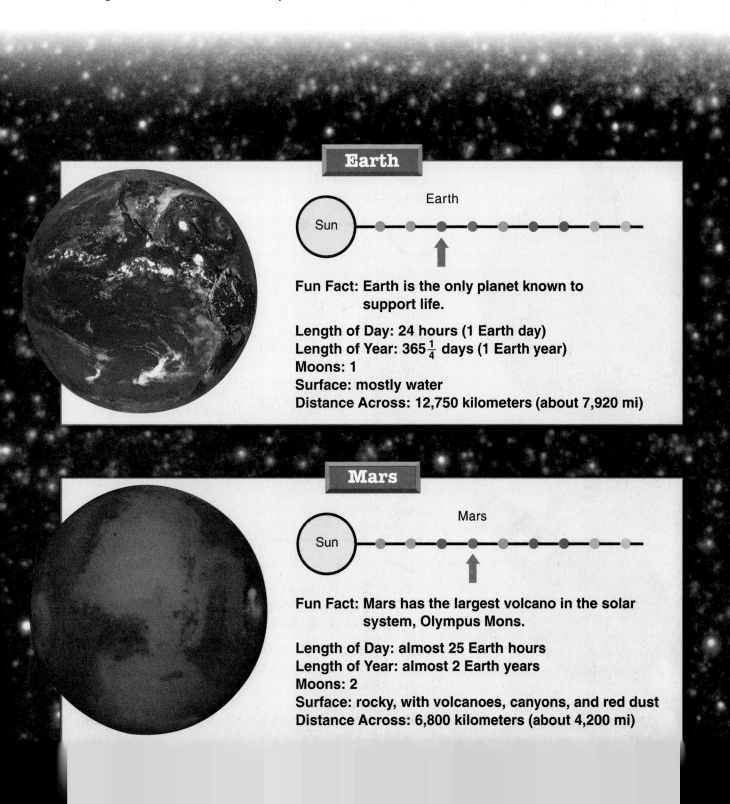

Earth

Earth

Sun

Fun Fact: Earth is the only planet known to support life.

Length of Day: 24 hours (1 Earth day)
Length of Year: $365\frac{1}{4}$ days (1 Earth year)
Moons: 1
Surface: mostly water
Distance Across: 12,750 kilometers (about 7,920 mi)

Mars

Mars

Sun

Fun Fact: Mars has the largest volcano in the solar system, Olympus Mons.

Length of Day: almost 25 Earth hours
Length of Year: almost 2 Earth years
Moons: 2
Surface: rocky, with volcanoes, canyons, and red dust
Distance Across: 6,800 kilometers (about 4,200 mi)

The Outer Planets

The five planets farthest from the sun are called the outer planets. The outer planets are Jupiter, Saturn, Uranus, Neptune, and Pluto.

The outer planets are alike in many ways. They are made mostly of frozen gases. They are very far from the sun, so their surfaces are much colder than the inner planets. All but Pluto are much larger than the inner planets. Jupiter is the solar system's largest planet. It is more than 1,000 times larger than Earth. Most of the outer planets have many moons. Many also have rings of dust and ice around them.

Pluto is different from the other outer planets. It is the smallest planet in the solar system. It is smaller than Earth's moon.

✓ **List the outer planets in order from the sun.**

Jupiter

Sun   Jupiter

Fun Fact: Two Earth-sized circles could fit inside Jupiter's Great Red Spot, a huge hurricane-like storm on Jupiter's surface.

Length of Day: 10 Earth hours
Length of Year: about 12 Earth years
Moons: 16 known
Surface: no solid surface; cold, slushy gases
Distance Across: 143,000 kilometers (about 88,900 mi)

Saturn

Sun   Saturn

Fun Fact: Saturn has a large system of rings that reaches 416,000 kilometers (260,000 mi) from its surface.

Length of Day: about 10 Earth hours
Length of Year: 29 Earth years
Moons: 18 known
Surface: frozen gases
Distance Across: 120,000 kilometers (about 75,000 mi)

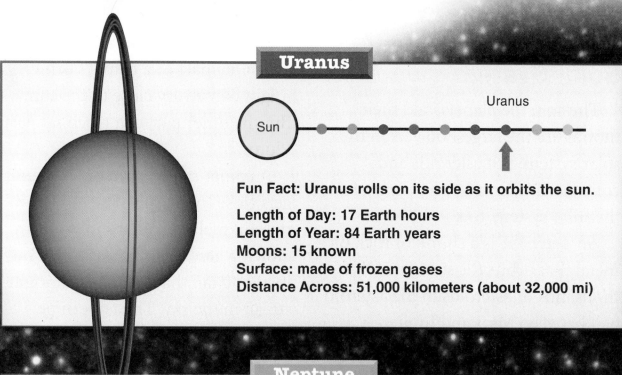

Uranus

Uranus

Sun

Fun Fact: Uranus rolls on its side as it orbits the sun.

Length of Day: 17 Earth hours
Length of Year: 84 Earth years
Moons: 15 known
Surface: made of frozen gases
Distance Across: 51,000 kilometers (about 32,000 mi)

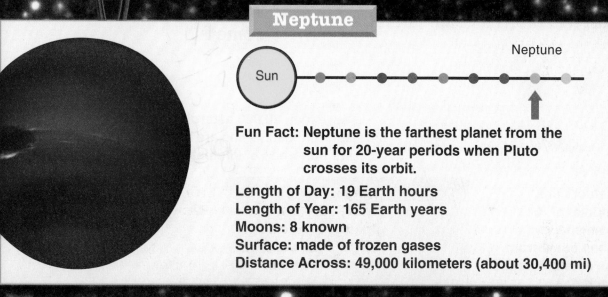

Neptune

Neptune

Sun

Fun Fact: Neptune is the farthest planet from the sun for 20-year periods when Pluto crosses its orbit.

Length of Day: 19 Earth hours
Length of Year: 165 Earth years
Moons: 8 known
Surface: made of frozen gases
Distance Across: 49,000 kilometers (about 30,400 mi)

Pluto

Pluto

Sun

Fun Fact: Pluto is made of ice. It has a moon almost as large as it is.

Length of Day: 6 Earth days
Length of Year: 248 Earth years
Moons: 1
Surface: made of frozen gases
Distance Across: 2300 kilometers (about 1,500 mi)

Other Bodies in the Solar System

The sun, the planets, and their moons are the largest objects in the solar system. But asteroids and comets, while smaller, are parts of the solar system, too.

An **asteroid** is a chunk of rock or metal that orbits the sun. There are thousands of asteroids in the asteroid belt between Mars and Jupiter.

A **comet** is a large ball of ice and dust that orbits the sun. The orbit of a comet is shaped like a large, flat oval. One part of a comet's orbit might come very close to the sun. But the other part can reach far past Pluto.

A comet can be seen only when it gets close to the sun. The heat from the sun melts a comet's ice to form glowing gases. The gases stream out in a long tail that looks like a bright streak in the sky. The tail can be millions of kilometers long.

✔ **What are asteroids and comets?**

More than 20,000 asteroids are in the asteroid belt. Some are small. Others are hundreds of kilometers wide. ▼

Meteors are chunks of rock from space. Many come from the asteroid belt. Each day, hundreds of meteors enter Earth's atmosphere. Those that don't burn up hit the surface and are called meteorites. ▼

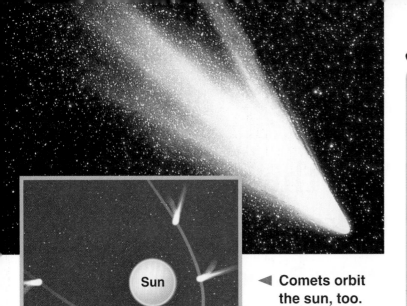

Sun

◄ Comets orbit the sun, too. Halley's comet can be seen from Earth every 76 years.

Summary

The solar system has nine planets that orbit the sun. Earth is one of those planets. Asteroids and comets are also parts of the solar system.

Review

1. What is a planet?
2. List three ways the inner planets are alike.
3. List three ways the outer planets are alike.
4. **Critical Thinking** How are asteroids and meteorites alike? How are they different?
5. **Test Prep** A comet is visible in the sky only when it is close to —
   A the sun
   B Earth
   C Mars
   D Pluto

LINKS

MATH LINK

How Many Moons? Make a bar graph showing the number of moons each planet has. How does the number of Earth's moons compare with the number of moons of other planets?

WRITING LINK

Narrative Writing—Story Pick a planet. Write a story for your teacher that tells what life would be like on that planet. Describe what it might be like to visit there. Share your story with your classmates.

HEALTH LINK

Sun Safety The sun's rays can harm the skin. That's why people use sunscreen. Sunscreens have an SPF number. Find out what *SPF* means. What SPF number sunscreen should you wear every day to protect you from the sun?

TECHNOLOGY LINK

Learn more about Mars by viewing *Mars Pathfinder Discovery* on the **Harcourt Science Newsroom Video**.

CNN
Turner
Le@rning

What Causes Earth's Seasons?

In this lesson, you can . . .

INVESTIGATE how Earth's tilt causes seasons.

LEARN ABOUT the seasons.

LINK to math, writing, art, and technology.

INVESTIGATE

How the Sun Strikes Earth

Activity Purpose Many places on Earth are hot in summer and cold in winter. In this investigation you will find out why. You will **compare** the way light rays strike a surface. Then you will **infer** how this affects Earth's temperatures.

Materials

- clear tape
- graph paper
- large book
- flashlight
- meterstick
- black marker
- wooden block
- red marker

Activity Procedure

1 Tape the graph paper to the book.

2 Hold the flashlight about 50 cm above the book. Shine the light straight down. The beam will make a circle on the paper. If the circle is bigger than the paper, bring the light closer.

◀ The leaves of some trees turn red, orange, and gold in the fall.

3. Have a partner use the black marker to draw around the light beam on the paper. (Picture A)

4. **Observe** the brightness of the light on the squares. **Record** your observations.

5. Keep the flashlight in the same position. Have a partner put the block under one end of the book and use the red marker to draw around the light on the paper. (Picture B)

6. **Observe** the brightness on the squares again. **Record** your observations.

Picture A

Draw Conclusions

1. How many squares are inside the black line? How many squares are inside the red line?

2. Inside which line was the light brighter?

3. **Scientists at Work** Scientists **compare** things to find out how they are the same and how they are different. Compare the results of Steps 3 and 5 of the investigation. Do straight light rays or tilted light rays give stronger light? Suppose the paper is Earth's surface. The light is the sun. Which area would have warmer weather? Explain.

Investigate Further **Predict** what will happen if the book is tilted even more. Test your prediction.

Picture B

Process Skill Tip

When you **compare**, you **observe** the properties of two or more things to see how they are alike and how they are different.

D67

The Seasons

FIND OUT

- why there are seasons
- what causes day and night

VOCABULARY

rotation
axis
revolution

How Earth Moves in Space

You are sitting reading this book. It seems like you are still. But you're not. Earth is traveling through space at almost 107,800 kilometers (67,000 mi) per hour. You are moving with Earth. You are also flying around the solar system as Earth orbits the sun.

Earth moves in two ways. First, Earth spins like a top. This is called rotation. **Rotation** (roh•TAY•shuhn) is the spinning of an object on its axis. Earth's **axis** (AK•sis) is an imaginary line that goes through the North Pole and the South Pole. Earth rotates on its axis once every 24 hours. One rotation takes one day.

Earth also circles the sun. This is called revolution. A **revolution** (rev•uh•LOO•shuhn) is the movement of one object around another object. Earth makes one revolution around the sun every $365\frac{1}{4}$ days. One revolution takes one year.

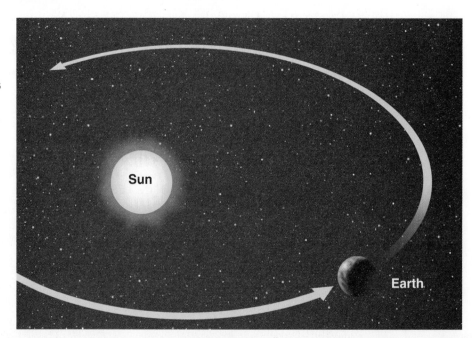

Earth rotates on its axis as it revolves around the sun. ▶

Sun

Earth

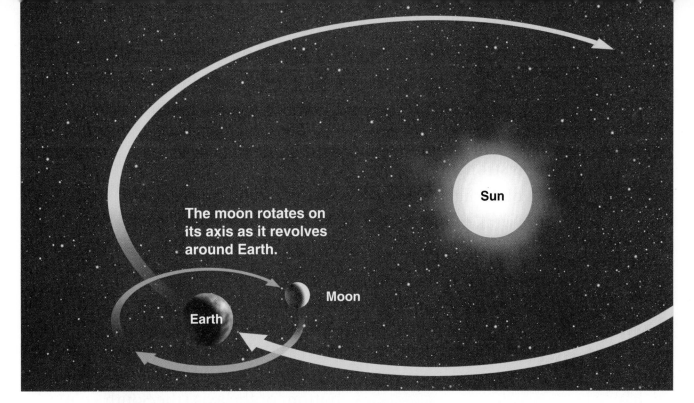

The moon rotates on its axis as it revolves around Earth.

Sun

Moon

Earth

▲ Both Earth and the moon rotate. The Earth rotates once a day. The moon rotates about once a month.

The moon also rotates and revolves. It rotates on its axis. It revolves around Earth. A day on the moon, or one rotation, is about 29 Earth days long. The moon takes this same amount of time to revolve around Earth.

Objects on Earth cast shadows. Shadows can help us observe Earth's rotation. As Earth rotates, the sun's position seems to change in the sky. But it is really the Earth that is moving.

In the morning the sun seems low in the sky. Objects cast long shadows. As the Earth rotates, the sun seems to move higher in the sky. Shadows get shorter. At noon, the sun is overhead. Objects cast short shadows—or no shadows at all. As Earth continues to rotate, the sun looks lower in the sky again. Shadows get longer until the sun sets.

✔ **What is rotation?**

Shadows are short at noon. They're longer at 2:00 P.M. because the sun is lower in the sky. ▼

What Causes Seasons

In most places on Earth, summer and winter are different. Summer is hot. There are many hours of daylight. Sunlight is strong. Winter is cold. The hours of daylight are shorter. Sunlight is weaker. Summer and winter are two seasons.

Earth has seasons because its axis is tilted. This means Earth is tipped to one side, like the book in the investigation was tilted. The tilt changes the way sunlight hits Earth at different times of the year. Sometimes the sun's rays are almost straight when they hit Earth's surface. At other times the sun's rays are slanted. This changes the amount of light and heat the surface gets.

Earth's axis is always pointing the same way in space. But because Earth is moving, the axis changes position compared with the position of the sun.

For part of the year the top of the axis (the North Pole) points in the direction of the sun. When Earth is in this position, it is summer in the northern half. During that time the bottom of the axis (the South Pole) points away from the sun. When Earth is in this position, it is winter in the southern half.

Earth has a curved surface. Some sunlight hits the surface straight on. Some sunlight hits the surface on a slant. ▼

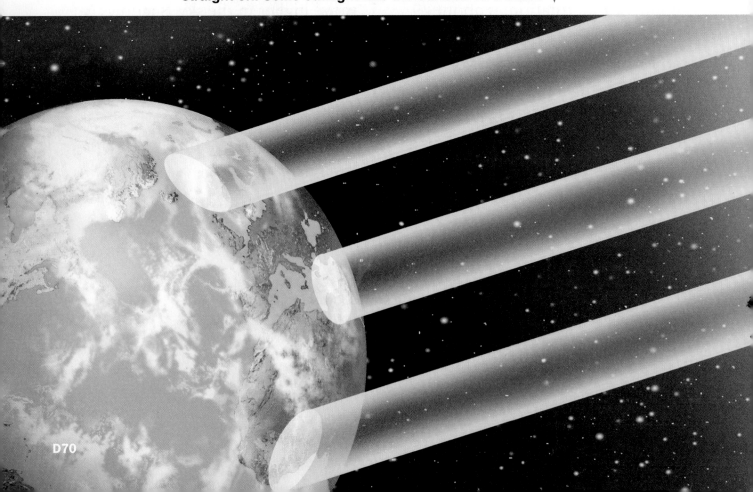

Spring

Summer

Winter

Fall.

Whichever end of Earth's axis points in the direction of the sun, the sun shines more directly on that part of Earth. This direct sunlight heats the ground and the air. It is summer.

Earth is always moving around the sun. Three months after summer starts, the top of the axis is not pointing in the direction of the sun anymore. Neither is the bottom of the axis. Days and nights are of equal length. Both the top half and the bottom half of the Earth get the same amount of light. Temperatures are cooler than in summer and warmer than in winter. It is fall in the northern half.

Three months later the northern half of the Earth points away from the sun. The sun shines less directly on its surface. Rays are slanted. Slanted rays cover a larger area, so the ground and the air are heated less. This makes the northern half of the Earth colder. It is winter.

Another three months pass. Again neither axis points in the direction of the sun. Days and nights are almost equal in length. Now it is spring. A full year has passed. Then the cycle starts again with summer.

Seasons in the northern and southern halves of Earth are reversed. When the northern half of Earth has spring, the southern half has fall. When the northern half has winter, the southern half has summer. Australia is on the southern half of Earth. So in Australia December is in the middle of summer. July is in the middle of winter.

✔ **Why are there seasons?**

What Causes Day and Night

It's 4:00 P.M. Your family decides to call a friend in Asia. When your dad makes the call, he wakes up your Asian friend. He was sleeping. It's the middle of the night there.

As you move from place to place on Earth, time changes. When you are eating dinner, people on the other side of the world might be having breakfast.

▲ When it is day in Chicago, Illinois, . . .

. . . it is night in Hong Kong, China. Hong Kong is on the other side of Earth from Chicago. ▼

Sunlight always shines on half of Earth. The other half is in darkness. ▼

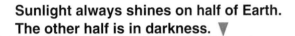

Sun

Earth's rotation causes this difference in time. At any one time, half of Earth is in sunlight. The other half is in darkness. The half in sunlight has day. The half in darkness has night.

✔ **How much of Earth's surface is in sunlight at one time?**

Summary

Earth rotates on its axis and revolves around the sun. Earth has seasons because its axis is tilted. The sun heats Earth's surface differently at different times of the year. Night and day happen as Earth rotates. Places on Earth's surface move from sunlight into darkness and back.

Review

1. What is a revolution?
2. When it is winter in the northern half of Earth, what season is it in the southern half?
3. Why are many places warmer in summer than in winter?
4. **Critical Thinking** How would day and night be different if Earth did not rotate?
5. **Test Prep** The tilt of Earth's axis causes —

   A rotation

   B day and night

   C seasons

   D sunlight

LINKS

MATH LINK

Measuring Shadows Put a stick in the ground. Measure the length of its shadow each hour. How does the shadow change? How could you use this shadow as a clock?

WRITING LINK

Persuasive Writing—Opinion Which is your favorite season? Write a paragraph for your family about why you like that season. Try to persuade them to agree with you.

ART LINK

Season Mobile Make a mobile about your favorite season. Include pictures or objects to show both things you see and activities you enjoy during that season.

TECHNOLOGY LINK

Learn more about seasons and other chapter topics by visiting this Internet Site.

www.scilinks.org/harcourt

SCiLINKS
THE WORLD'S A CLICK AWAY

How Do the Moon and Earth Interact?

In this lesson, you can . . .

 INVESTIGATE the phases of the moon.

 LEARN ABOUT why the moon seems to change.

 LINK to math, writing, literature, and technology.

 **INVESTIGATE**

The Moon's Phases

Activity Purpose If you look at the moon each night, you will see that its shape seems to change. These shapes are called *phases*. In this investigation you will **observe** how a light shining on a ball looks different as you move around the ball.

Materials
- lamp with no shade
- softball

Activity Procedure

1. Work with a partner. Turn on the lamp. Your teacher will darken the room.

2. Have Person 1 hold the ball and stand with his or her back to the lighted bulb. Hold the ball as shown. Continue holding the ball this way until the end of the procedure. (Picture A)

◀ You see the moon rise from Earth. But if you were on the moon, you would see Earth rise!

3 Have Person 2 stand in position 1 in Picture A. **Observe** the ball. Make a drawing of the ball's lighted side.

4 Person 2 now moves to position 2. Turn toward the ball. Make a drawing of the lighted part of the ball.

5 Have Person 2 move to position 3. Make a drawing of the lighted part of the ball.

6 Person 2 again moves. This time to position 4. Turn toward the ball. Make a drawing of the lighted part of the ball.

Picture A

7 Switch roles and repeat the procedure so Person 1 can observe the patterns of light on the ball.

Draw Conclusions

1. What part of the ball was lighted at each position?

2. The ball represents the moon. What does the light bulb represent? What represents a person viewing the moon from Earth?

3. **Scientists at Work** Scientists **use models** to make **inferences** to explain how things work. If the ball represents the moon, what can you infer that the different parts of the lighted ball represent?

Process Skill Tip

When you **observe** something, you use your senses to get information about it. When you **infer**, you use your observations to form an opinion.

How the Moon and Earth Interact

FIND OUT

- what the moon's phases are
- what causes eclipses

VOCABULARY

phase
lunar eclipse
solar eclipse

The Phases of the Moon

If you watch the moon for a month, its shape seems to change. Sometimes it looks like a big round ball. At other times you see a thin sliver. Why do these changes happen?

The half of the moon that faces the sun is always lighted. As the moon moves around Earth, different amounts of its lighted and dark sides face Earth. The moon's phase depends on the part of the lighted half you can see. **Phases** are the different shapes the moon seems to have in the sky.

It takes about one month for the moon to revolve around Earth. It takes the same amount of time for the moon to rotate. This causes the same side of the moon to always face Earth. ▶

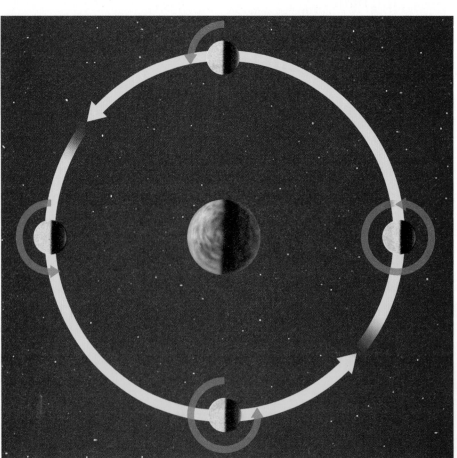

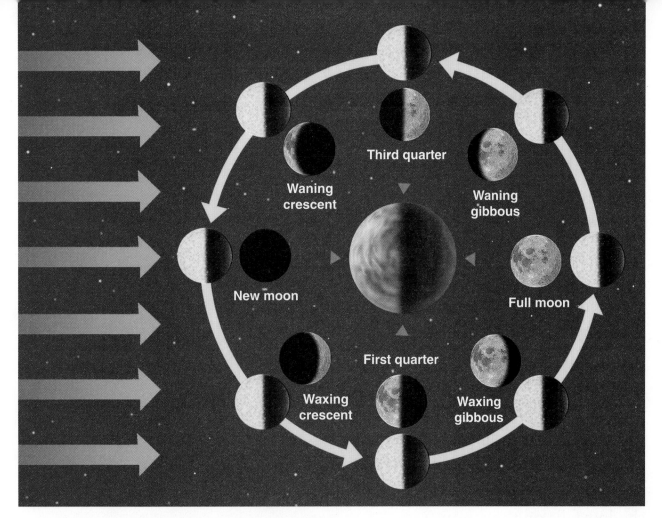

▲ The photographs show what the moon looks like from Earth. The drawings show what the moon would look like from space.

The moon goes through all of its phases every $29\frac{1}{2}$ days. During the phase called the new moon, the lighted half faces away from Earth. You can't see the moon at all. After the new moon, the moon seems to get bigger.

As the moon continues in its orbit around Earth, one lighted edge comes into view. This is a crescent moon. About one week after the new moon, half of the moon's lighted face can be seen. This is the first quarter. The next phase is the gibbous moon.

It shows a little less than $\frac{3}{4}$ of the moon's lighted side.

About two weeks after the new moon, you see the full moon. At full moon you can see the whole face of the moon. The moon has completed half of its orbit around Earth.

After the full moon, the phases reverse. The lighted part you see gets smaller. First you see the gibbous moon again. Then you see the third quarter. The last phase is another crescent moon.

✔ **What are the moon's phases?**

Eclipses of the Moon

Everything the sun shines on casts a shadow. Earth and the moon cast shadows, too. Most of the time these shadows fall on empty space. But sometimes these shadows can be seen from Earth's surface.

You know the moon revolves around Earth. At times the Earth is between the sun and moon. If the sun, Earth, and moon are in a straight line, Earth blocks some of the sun's light from falling on the moon. Although you should see a full moon, the moon gets dark for a time. This is called a lunar eclipse. A **lunar eclipse** happens when Earth's shadow falls on the moon.

✔ **What causes a lunar eclipse?**

When the sun shines on you, you cast a shadow. ▶

Sun

A total lunar eclipse causes all of the moon's face to look dark red. Total lunar eclipses do not happen as often as partial eclipses. This is because the sun, the Earth, and the moon need to be in a straight line for Earth's shadow to completely cover the moon.

A partial lunar eclipse blocks only part of the sun's light. Watching partial eclipses helped early scientists figure out that Earth is round. Why would eclipses help them see that Earth is round? ▼

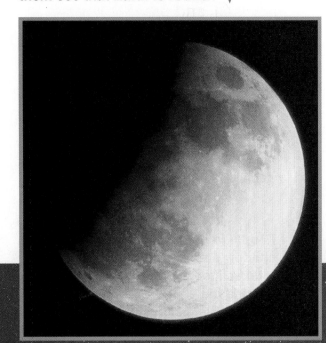

The sun shines on objects in space. They cast shadows, too. Sometimes Earth's shadow falls on the moon. This causes a lunar eclipse. ▼

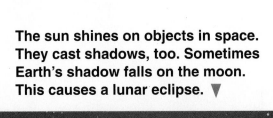

Earth

Moon

Eclipses of the Sun

A shadow slowly covers the sun. The whole sky turns dark in the middle of the day. Ancient peoples thought this was the end of the world. Today we know it's a solar eclipse. A **solar eclipse** happens when the moon's shadow falls on Earth. This happens when the moon moves between the Earth and the sun.

During a total solar eclipse, the moon blocks out the sun. Only a halo of sunlight remains around the moon. The areas where a total eclipse can be seen is small. Outside this area only part of the sun is covered.

✔ **What causes a solar eclipse?**

A total solar eclipse happens when the moon moves between Earth and the sun. These photos show what the sun looks like as a total solar eclipse takes place. Total solar eclipses are rare. ▶

People in the small shadow area see the total eclipse. Those outside the shadow see a partial eclipse. ▼

Sun

Summary

Phases are the different shapes the moon seems to have in the sky. The moon goes through its phases every $29\frac{1}{2}$ days. Eclipses happen when one object in space moves into the shadow of another. There are lunar eclipses and solar eclipses.

Review

1. Describe a new moon.
2. Compare and contrast a lunar and a solar eclipse.
3. What do you see from Earth during a total solar eclipse?
4. **Critical Thinking** Tell what phase the moon is in during a lunar eclipse. Explain your answer.
5. **Test Prep** Which of these is **NOT** a phase of the moon?

   A new   **C** crescent
   B full   **D** eclipse

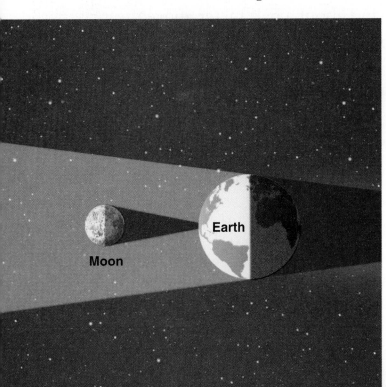

LINKS

MATH LINK

Sketch It Sketch the shape of the moon each night for one month. Start with the new moon. How much time does it take for all eight phases to take place? Predict the date of the next new moon.

WRITING LINK

Narrative Writing—Personal Story When the sun got dark in ancient times, people thought the sun was gone. Suppose that you lived then. You are seeing a solar eclipse. Write a story for a younger child to explain what you think is happening.

LITERATURE LINK

Find Out More Find out more about the sun, the moon, or eclipses by reading *The Sun and the Moon* by Patrick Moore.

TECHNOLOGY LINK

Learn more about interactions in space by investigating *Blast Off into Orbit* on **Harcourt Science Explorations CD-ROM.**

What Is Beyond the Solar System?

In this lesson, you can . . .

 INVESTIGATE star patterns.

 LEARN ABOUT the stars we see in the sky.

 LINK to math, writing, literature, and technology.

INVESTIGATE

Star Patterns

Activity Purpose Can you see patterns in the stars? People saw star patterns in ancient times. They saw horses, bears, and dragons in the sky. In this investigation you will make your own star pattern. Then you will **compare** the pattern to objects you know about.

Materials

- gummed stars
- black construction paper
- white crayon or chalk

Activity Procedure

1 Take the stars in your hand. Hold your hand about a half meter above the paper. Drop the stars onto the black paper. Glue the stars where they fall on the paper. (Picture A)

◄ Telescopes were invented many years ago. This telescope was used by scientists around the year 1620.

2 **Observe** the stars. Look for a picture that the stars make. Use the white crayon to connect the stars to show the picture or pattern. You can connect all of the stars or just some of them.

3 Trade star patterns with other people in your class. See if they can tell what your star pattern is.

Picture A

Draw Conclusions

1. People have looked at the stars for thousands of years. Different people have seen different pictures in the stars. Why do you think this is so?

2. Some people look at a star pattern and see different things. A star pattern that looks like a water dipper to one person might look like part of a bear to another person. Look again at the stars on your paper. What other patterns can you find in them?

3. **Scientists at Work** Scientists **compare** things to see how they are alike. In the investigation you compared your star pattern to objects you know about. What person, animal, or object does your star pattern look like?

Investigate Further **Observe** real star patterns. Choose a star pattern, and draw it as you see it with the unaided eye. Look at the star pattern again using binoculars or a telescope. Use another color to add anything to the pattern that you didn't see before. **Compare** what you saw in your two observations.

Process Skill Tip

When you **compare** things, you look for properties that are the same.

The Way We See Stars

Star Patterns

A **star** is a hot ball of glowing gases—like our sun. The stars you see at night are much like the sun, but they are farther away. This makes the stars look very small. It also makes the stars look like they are all the same distance from Earth. But they are not. Some stars are not too far from the solar system. Some are very, very far away.

FIND OUT

- what constellations are
- how telescopes help us see stars

VOCABULARY

star
constellation
telescope

Ursa Major Native Americans named the constellation shown here the Great Bear (Ursa Major). The seven stars highlighted inside the bear make up the Big Dipper. The people of ancient China thought the stars of the Big Dipper looked like a chariot. The chariot carried the king of the sky. ▼

Just as you did in the investigation, ancient people looked for patterns in the stars. Then they made up stories to explain the patterns. A group of stars that forms a pattern is a **constellation**. People all over the world looked at the same stars and saw different patterns.

✔ **What is a constellation?**

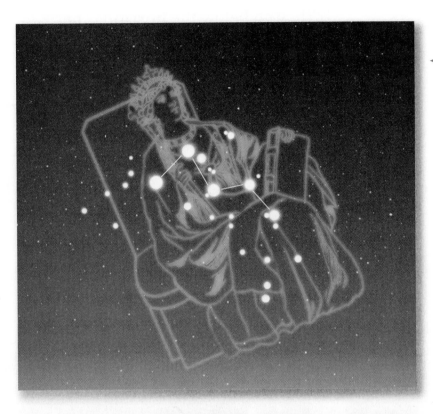

◀ **Cassiopeia** The people of ancient Greece called this constellation Cassiopeia. In the story they made up, Cassiopeia was the queen of part of Africa. She said that her daughter was more beautiful than anyone. Her bragging made one of the Greek gods angry. So he tried to take away Cassiopeia's daughter. A hero named Perseus saved the girl. But the angry god punished Cassiopeia. He turned her into a constellation.

◀ **Tayamni** This constellation was named by the Native American people called the Lakota. Tayamni means "the animal." The ancient Greeks had a different name for Tayamni. They called part of the same pattern Orion, the hunter. The three bright stars in the middle of Tayamni form the animal's back. The same stars form the belt of Orion.

Stars Seem to Move

Pick a constellation. Find it at the start of the evening and again later that night. You will see that it has moved. Stars don't really move around us. But they seem to move because Earth rotates. The spot where you are moves as Earth spins, so the stars above you change. Since Earth turns toward the east, the stars rise above the horizon in the east. As Earth keeps turning, the stars keep moving across the sky. When they finally get to the horizon in the west, they go below the horizon. They seem to disappear.

Stars and Seasons

This is the Big Dipper, part of the constellation Ursa Major. If you watch carefully, you can see how this constellation seems to move from place to place as the seasons change.

▲ In the spring, the Big Dipper is high in the sky. It looks upside down.

▲ In the summer, the Big Dipper has moved down in the sky. Its handle is pointing up.

You see different constellations at different times of the year. This is because Earth revolves around the sun. As Earth circles the sun, you see stars in different parts of space.

Polaris, or the North Star, is the only star that seems to stand still. The North Star is above Earth's axis.

The constellations near the North Star don't move across the sky. They just circle around the North Star. The Big Dipper is a constellation that circles the North Star.

✔ **Why do stars seem to move across the sky?**

▲ **In the fall, the Big Dipper is low in the sky. It looks as if it could hold water.**

▲ **In the winter, the Big Dipper has moved up in the sky. Its handle is pointing down.**

Observing Stars

People have looked at the stars for thousands of years. But many stars were not bright enough for people to see until the invention of the telescope. A **telescope** makes things that are far away look clearer and bigger. Many more stars can be seen with the telescope than with the unaided eye.

The astronomer Galileo used one of the first telescopes. He saw Saturn's rings through it in the early 1600s. Galileo's telescope made things look about 30 times as close as they are. Now telescopes can make things look thousands of times as close.

✔ **What does a telescope do?**

To see stars, you look through the eyepiece.

This piece helps you point the telescope to the right spot.

Light from the stars goes through this tube to the eyepiece.

Light enters the telescope here. It goes through a lens. The bigger this lens is, the larger the stars look.

The telescope stands on three legs. The legs are called a tripod. The tripod holds the telescope still while you use it.

▲ Some binoculars are made to look at the stars. Like telescopes, they make faraway things look bigger. Most of them aren't as powerful as telescopes, but they are easier to use and carry.

Summary

Constellations are groups of stars that form patterns. A telescope is a tool that makes faraway things look clearer and bigger. More stars can be seen with a telescope than without one.

Review

1. What is a star?

2. In which direction do most constellations move in the sky?

3. How do the number of stars you can see without a telescope compare to the number you can see with a telescope?

4. **Critical Thinking** Why might different people see different patterns in the same stars?

5. **Test Prep** Stars seem to move across the sky each night because —

   A they orbit Earth

   B they are bright

   C Earth rotates

   D Earth is tilted

LINKS

MATH LINK

Star Track Pick a constellation. Find it in the night sky. Draw its position each week on a sheet of paper. After three months, look at your results. Use arrows to show the constellation's movement. How did it move?

WRITING LINK

Expressive Writing—Poem Write a poem about the night sky. What does it look like? How does it make you feel? Share your poem with classmates.

LITERATURE LINK

Studying Stars What are stars like? How did they form? How do they change? Find out in *The Stars: Light in the Night Sky* by Jeanne Bendick.

TECHNOLOGY LINK

Visit the Harcourt Learning Site for related links, activities, and resources.

www.harcourtschool.com

WELCOME TO **THE LEARNING SITE**

Sky Watchers

For centuries people around the world observed the night sky by using only their eyes. These sky watchers made detailed observations and charted what they saw. They used the information they gathered to decide when to plant their crops or to take journeys.

Early Observatories

The Anasazi of North America were one of the cultures that made early observatories. An Anasazi observatory has been found in New Mexico.

In England there is a group of huge stones called Stonehenge. The stones are set in a circle in a way that would allow risings and settings of the sun and the moon to be tracked. Scientists and historians hypothesize that Stonehenge is a giant calendar made of rocks.

The First Telescopes

With the use of lenses to make telescopes, people learned much more about the night sky. Galileo, a scientist in Italy, read about the telescope and made his own. It could magnify objects 20 or 30 times. From his observations, Galileo made inferences about the objects in the

The History of Astronomy

1400 B.C.
Stonehenge is completed.

1608
Hans Lippershey produces the first telescope.

1947
Mount Palomar observatory is completed.

1500 B.C. 1500 1600 1700 1800 1900

1543
Copernicus publishes his book stating that the sun is the center of the universe.

1610
Galileo observes Jupiter's moons.

sky. He even saw moons orbiting Jupiter.

Modern Telescopes

During the twentieth century, bigger and bigger telescopes were designed. These telescopes use mirrors instead of lenses. The larger the mirror, the more detail in the image it produces. One of the newest of these telescopes is at the Keck Observatory at the top of Mauna Kea, Hawai'i. At 10 meters (400 in.) across, the two Keck telescopes have the largest mirrors of any telescopes in the world.

Radio telescopes have made it possible to explore space day or night, rain or shine. That's because these telescopes pick up radio waves instead of light. The largest radio telescope is near Arecibo in Puerto Rico. In New Mexico, the Very Large Array is made up of 27 radio telescope antennas, each one measuring 25 meters (82 ft) across.

Scientists are always trying to find better ways of observing the night sky. They've even put a telescope in space. The Hubble Space Telescope orbits high above the atmosphere of Earth. Without the atmosphere to look through, it can make clearer pictures than ground-based telescopes.

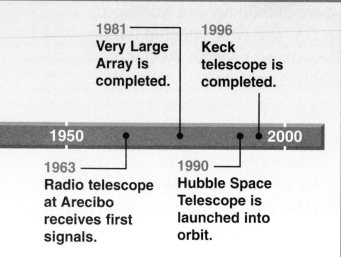

1981
Very Large Array is completed.

1996
Keck telescope is completed.

1950   2000

1963
Radio telescope at Arecibo receives first signals.

1990
Hubble Space Telescope is launched into orbit.

Think About It

1. Why would people in ancient civilizations be interested in the stars and planets?

2. Why does the Hubble Space Telescope take clearer pictures than telescopes on Earth?

Mae Jemison

ASTRONAUT, PHYSICIAN, BIOMEDICAL ENGINEER

"I want to make sure we use all our talent, not just 25 percent."

Mae Jemison was the first African-American woman in space. She was a mission specialist on the 1992 *Endeavour* space shuttle flight. Before the flight, she helped check the shuttle, its computer software, and the tiles that protect the ship from burning up when returning to Earth.

For Jemison, becoming an astronaut was a childhood dream come true. She began her career by going to medical school. While a student, she traveled to Thailand, Cuba, and Kenya to offer medical help. She joined the Peace Corps after graduating from medical school. She spent two years in West Africa.

Jemison returned to the United States and became a doctor in Los Angeles. She applied to the National Aeronautics and Space Administration (NASA) to be an astronaut. She was not accepted the first time she applied. She applied again and was accepted. After five years of training and working at NASA, she was selected for the *Endeavour* mission. All her hard work had paid off!

Think About It

1. How could living in a foreign country help a person get ready for a trip in outer space?
2. How can studying in school help a person make his or her dreams come true?

Earth Model

Why do we have seasons?

Materials
- Styrofoam ball
- two pencils
- flashlight

Procedure
1. Stick a pencil through the middle of the ball. This represents Earth's axis.

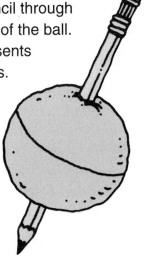

2. With the other pencil, draw a line around the middle of the ball. This is the equator. Put the Earth on a table. The axis should lean to the right.

3. Shine the flashlight on the left side of the Earth. The light represents the sun. Place the light about 13 cm away. Observe where the light rays hit the ball.

4. Shine the light on the right side of the Earth. Where do the light rays hit the ball? Compare how the light hits the ball each time.

Draw Conclusions
How does this explain seasons in the northern half of the Earth?

A Look at Rotation

How does day become night?

Materials
- a small self-stick note
- spinning Earth globe
- flashlight

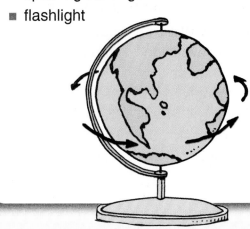

Procedure
1. Write where you live on the self-stick note. Place the note on your state on the globe.

2. Shine the flashlight on the globe. Your teacher will then turn off the lights.

3. Slowly spin the globe counterclockwise.

Draw Conclusions
What happens to the place where you put your note? What does this represent?

Chapter 3 Review and Test Preparation

Vocabulary Review

Use the terms below to complete the sentences 1 through 14. The page numbers in ( ) tell you where to look in the chapter if you need help.

solar system (D58)	**revolution** (D68)
orbit (D58)	**phases** (D76)
planet (D58)	**lunar eclipse** (D78)
asteroid (D64)	**solar eclipse** (D80)
comet (D64)	**star** (D84)
rotation (D68)	**constellation** (D85)
axis (D68)	**telescope** (D88)

1. A large body of rock or gas that orbits the sun is a ___.

2. An ___ is a chunk of rock or metal that orbits the sun.

3. When the moon's shadow falls on Earth we see a ___.

4. A ___ makes faraway things look clearer and bigger.

5. The spinning of an object on its axis is called ___.

6. A ___ is a large ball of ice and dust that orbits the sun.

7. The moon has ___ that make it seem to change shape.

8. A ___ is a group of stars that forms a pattern.

9. Earth has an imaginary line, or ___, that runs through the North Pole and the South Pole.

10. The movement of one object around another object is called ___.

11. The ___ is made up of the sun and all the objects that orbit around it.

12. An ___ is the path of an object as it moves around another object in space.

13. When Earth's shadow falls on the moon, we see a ___.

14. A ___ is a ball of hot, glowing gases.

Connect Concepts

The motions of the Earth and the moon cause certain things to happen. Choose a term below to fill in the chart and complete each sentence.

day and night	**seasons**
lunar eclipses	**solar eclipses**
phases	**years**

Motions of the Earth and the Moon	
Earth's tilt	causes 15. ___.
Earth's rotation	causes 16. ___.
Earth's revolution	causes 17. ___.
Earth's shadow	causes 18. ___.
The moon's shadow	causes 19. ___.
The moon's movement	causes 20. ___.

Check Understanding

Write the letter of the best choice.

21. The outer planets are —
    A like Earth
    B Mars and Jupiter
    C mostly larger than Earth
    D made of rock

22. Two revolutions of Earth take —
    F two days   H two months
    G two weeks   J two years

23. When the moon looks like a lighted circle in the sky, it is in the ___ phase.
    A full moon
    B new moon
    C crescent moon
    D gibbous moon

Critical Thinking

24. In what ways is Pluto like an inner planet?

25. How would Earth be different if its axis were not tilted?

Process Skills Review

26. You can use distance from the sun to classify planets. Some are inner planets. Some are outer planets. **Classify** the inner planets as those *with moons* and those *without moons*.

27. **Compare** the revolutions of the moon and Earth. How are they alike? How are they different?

28. It is always cold at the North Pole. What can you **infer** about the way the sun's rays hit the North Pole?

Performance Assessment

Ordering Planets

Use the table to put the planets in order from largest to smallest based on their mass. Record your results. Then sort the planets into two groups, those with rings and those without rings. Compare your lists. What conclusions can you draw by organizing this data?

Planet	Mass of Planet (The mass of Mercury = 1.)	Planet Has Rings?
Earth	17	no
Jupiter	5300	yes
Mars	2	no
Mercury	1	no
Neptune	288	yes
Pluto	$\frac{1}{5}$	no
Saturn	1587	yes
Uranus	243	yes
Venus	14	no

Unit Project Wrap Up

Here are some ideas for ways to wrap up your unit project.

Display at a Science Fair

Display the results of your project in a school science fair. Prepare a written report describing the procedure you used and your results. Display the data you collected.

Make Weather Predictions

Use the weather information you gather to make predictions about weather. Compare your predictions with the actual weather.

Make a Weather Map

Learn about the symbols shown on weather maps. Then make your own map showing weather patterns in the United States on one day.

Investigate Further

How could you make your project better? What other questions do you have? Plan ways to find answers to your questions. Use the Science Handbook on pages R2-R9 for help.

References

Science Handbook

Planning an Investigation

When scientists observe something they want to study, they use scientific inquiry to plan and conduct their study. They use science process skills as tools to help them gather, organize, analyze, and present their information. This plan will help you work like a scientist.

Step 1—Observe and ask questions.

Which food does my hamster eat the most of?

- Use your senses to make observations.
- Record a question you would like to answer.

Step 2—Make a hypothesis.

My hypothesis: My hamster will eat more sunflower seeds than any other food.

- Choose one possible answer, or hypothesis, to your question.
- Write your hypothesis in a complete sentence.
- Think about what investigation you can do to test your hypothesis.

Step 3—Plan your test.

I'll give my hamster equal amounts of three kinds of foods, then observe what she eats.

- Write down the steps you will follow to do your test. Decide how to conduct a fair test by controlling variables.
- Decide what equipment you will need.
- Decide how you will gather and record your data.

Step 4 — Conduct your test.

I'll repeat this experiment for four days. I'll meaure how much food is left each time.

- Follow the steps you wrote.
- Observe and measure carefully.
- Record everything that happens.
- Organize your data so that you can study it carefully.

Step 5 — Draw conclusions and share results.

My hypothesis was correct. She ate more sunflower seeds than the other kinds of foods.

- Analyze the data you gathered.
- Make charts, graphs, or tables to show your data.
- Write a conclusion. Describe the evidence you used to determine whether your test supported your hypothesis.
- Decide whether your hypothesis was correct.

Investigate Further

I wonder if there are other foods she will eat . . .

Using Science Tools

Using a Hand Lens

1. Hold the hand lens about 12 centimeters (5 in.) from your eye.

2. Bring the object toward you until it comes into focus.

Using a Thermometer

1. Place the thermometer in the liquid. Never stir the liquid with the thermometer. Don't touch the thermometer any more than you need to. If you are measuring the temperature of the air, make sure that the thermometer is not in line with a direct light source.

2. Move so that your eyes are even with the liquid in the thermometer.

3. If you are measuring a material that is not being heated or cooled, wait about two minutes for the reading to become stable, or stay the same. Find the scale line that meets the top of the liquid in the thermometer, and read the temperature.

4. If the material you are measuring is being heated or cooled, you will not be able to wait before taking your measurements. Measure as quickly as you can.

Caring for and Using a Microscope

Caring for a Microscope

- Carry a microscope with two hands.
- Never touch any of the lenses of a microscope with your fingers.

Using a Microscope

1. Raise the eyepiece as far as you can using the coarse-adjustment knob. Place your slide on the stage.

2. Start by using the lowest power. The lowest-power lens is usually the shortest. Place the lens in the lowest position it can go to without touching the slide.

3. Look through the eyepiece, and begin adjusting it upward with the coarse-adjustment knob. When the slide is close to being in focus, use the fine-adjustment knob.

4. When you want to use a higher-power lens, first focus the slide under low power. Then, watching carefully to make sure that the lens will not hit the slide, turn the higher-power lens into place. Use only the fine-adjustment knob when looking through the higher-power lens.

You may use a Brock microscope. This sturdy microscope has only one lens.

1. Place the object to be viewed on the stage.

2. Look through the eyepiece, and raise the tube until the object comes into focus.

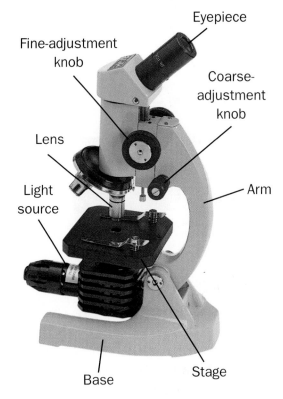

A Light Microscope

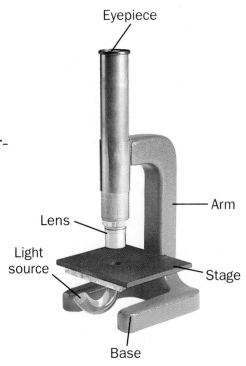

A Brock Microscope

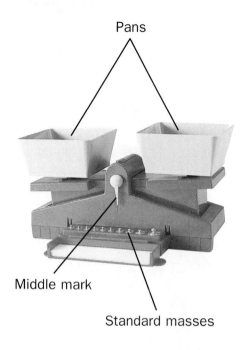

Pans

Middle mark

Standard masses

Using a Balance

1. Look at the pointer on the base to make sure the empty pans are balanced. Place the object you wish to measure in the left-hand pan.

2. Add the standard masses to the other pan. As you add masses, you should see the pointer move. When the pointer is at the middle mark, the pans are balanced.

3. Add the numbers on the masses you used. The total is the mass in grams of the object you measured.

Using a Spring Scale

Measuring an Object at Rest

1. Hook the spring scale to the object.

2. Lift the scale and object with a smooth motion. Do not jerk them upward.

3. Wait until any motion of the spring comes to a stop. Then read the number of newtons from the scale.

Measuring an Object in Motion

1. With the object resting on a table, hook the spring scale to it.

2. Pull the object smoothly across the table. Do not jerk the object.

3. As you pull, read the number of newtons you are using to pull the object.

Measuring Liquids

Beaker   **Graduate**

1. Pour the liquid you want to measure into a measuring container. Put your measuring container on a flat surface, with the measuring scale facing you.

2. Look at the liquid through the container. Move so that your eyes are even with the surface of the liquid in the container.

3. To read the volume of the liquid, find the scale line that is even with the surface of the liquid.

4. If the surface of the liquid is not exactly even with a line, estimate the volume of the liquid. Decide which line the liquid is closer to, and use that number.

Using a Ruler or Meterstick

1. Place the zero mark or end of the ruler or meterstick next to one end of the distance or object you want to measure.

2. On the ruler or meterstick, find the place next to the other end of the distance or object.

3. Look at the scale on the ruler or meterstick. This will show the distance or the length of the object.

Using a Timing Device

1. Reset the stopwatch to zero.

2. When you are ready to begin timing, press *Start*.

3. As soon as you are ready to stop timing, press *Stop*.

4. The numbers on the dial or display show how many minutes, seconds, and parts of seconds have passed.

Using a Computer

Writing Reports

To write a report with a computer, use a word processing software program. After you are in the program, type your report. By using certain keys and the mouse, you can control how the words look, move words, delete or add words and copy them, check your spelling, and print your report.

Save your work to the desktop or hard disk of the computer, or to a floppy disk. You can go back to your saved work later if you want to revise it.

There are many reasons for revising your work. You may find new information to add or mistakes you want to correct. You may want to change the way you report your information because of who will read it.

Computers make revising easy. You delete what you don't want, add the new parts, and then save. You can also save different versions of your work.

For a science lab report, it is important to show the same kinds of information each time. With a computer, you can make a general format for a lab report, save the format, and then use it again and again.

Making Graphs and Charts

You can make a graph or chart with most word processing software programs. You can also use special software programs such as Data ToolKit or Graph Links. With Graph Links you can make pictographs and circle, bar, line, and double-line graphs.

First, decide what kind of graph or chart will best communicate your data. Sometimes it's easiest to do this by sketching your ideas on paper. Then you can decide what format and categories you need for your graph or chart. Choose that format for the program. Then type your information. Most software programs include a tutor that gives you step-by-step directions for making a graph or chart.

Doing Research

Computers can help you find current information from all over the world through the Internet. The Internet connects thousands of computer sites that have been set up by schools, libraries, museums, and many other organizations.

Get permission from an adult before you log on to the Internet. Find out the rules for Internet use at school or at home. Then log on and go to a search engine, which will help you find what you need. Type in keywords, words that tell the subject of your search.If you get too much information that isn't exactly about the topic,

make your keywords more specific. When you find the information you need, save it or print it.

Harcourt Science tells you about many Internet sites related to what you are studying. To find out about these sites, called Web sites, look for Technology Links in the lessons in this book.

If you need to contact other people to help in your research, you can use e-mail. Log into your e-mail program, type the address of the person you want to reach, type your message, and send it. Be sure to have adult permission before sending or receiving e-mail.

Another way to use a computer for research is to access CD-ROMs. These are discs that look like music CDs. CD-ROMs can hold huge amounts of data, including words, still pictures, audio, and video. Encyclopedias, dictionaries, almanacs, and other sources of information are available on CD-ROMs. These computer discs are valuable resources for your research.

Glossary

This Glossary contains important science words and their definitions. Each word is respelled as it would be in a dictionary. When you see the ' mark after a syllable, pronounce that syllable with more force than the other syllables. The page number at the end of the definition tells where to find the word in your book. The boldfaced letters in the examples in the Pronunciation Key that follows show how these letters are pronounced in the respellings after each glossary word.

PRONUNCIATION KEY

a	add, map	m	move, seem	u	up, done
ā	ace, rate	n	nice, tin	û(r)	burn, term
â(r)	care, air	ng	ring, song	yōō	fuse, few
ä	palm, father	o	odd, hot	v	vain, eve
b	bat, rub	ō	open, so	w	win, away
ch	check, catch	ô	order, jaw	y	yet, yearn
d	dog, rod	oi	oil, boy	z	zest, muse
e	end, pet	ou	pout, now	zh	vision, pleasure
ē	equal, tree	ŏŏ	took, full	ə	the schwa, an
f	fit, half	ōō	pool, food		unstressed vowel
g	go, log	p	pit, stop		representing the
h	hope, hate	r	run, poor		sound spelled
i	it, give	s	see, pass		*a* in *above*
ī	ice, write	sh	sure, rush		*e* in *sicken*
j	joy, ledge	t	talk, sit		*i* in *possible*
k	cool, take	th	thin, both		*o* in *melon*
l	look, rule	t͟h	this, bathe		*u* in *circus*

Other symbols:

- • separates words into syllables
- ' indicates heavier stress on a syllable
- ' indicates light stress on a syllable

A

absorption [ab·sôrp′shən] The stopping of light **(F40)**

amphibian [am·fib′ē·ən] An animal that begins life in the water and moves onto land as an adult **(A50)**

anemometer [an′ə·mom′ə·tər] An instrument that measures wind speed **(D40)**

asteroid [as′tər·oid] A chunk of rock that orbits the sun **(D64)**

atmosphere [at′məs·fir′] The air that surrounds Earth **(D30)**

atom [at′əm] The basic building block of matter **(E16)**

axis [ak′sis] An imaginary line that goes through the North Pole and the South Pole of Earth **(D68)**

B

barrier island [bar′ē·ər i′lənd] A landform; a thin island along a coast **(C35)**

bird [bûrd] An animal that has feathers, two legs, and wings **(A45)**

C

canyon [kan′yən] A landform; a deep valley with very steep sides **(C35)**

chemical change [kem′i·kəl chānj′] A change that forms different kinds of matter **(E46)**

chlorophyll [klôr′ə·fil′] The substance that gives plants their green color; it helps a plant use energy from the sun to make food **(A20)**

clay [klā] A type of soil made up of very small grains; it holds water well **(C69)**

coastal forest [kōs′təl fôr′ist] A thick forest with tall trees that gets a lot of rain and does not get very warm or cold **(B15)**

comet [kom′it] A large ball of ice and dust that orbits the sun **(D64)**

community [kə·myoō′nə·tē] All the populations of organisms that live in an ecosystem **(B7)**

condensation [kon′dən·sā′shən] The changing of a gas into a liquid **(D17)**

conductor [kən·duk′tər] A material in which thermal energy moves easily **(F15)**

coniferous forest [kō·nif′ər·əs fôr′ist] A forest in which most of the trees are conifers (cone-bearing) and stay green all year **(B16)**

conservation [kon′ser·vā′shən] The saving of resources by using them carefully **(C76)**

constellation [kon′stə•lā′shən] A group of stars that form a pattern **(D84)**

consumer [kən•sōōm′ər] A living thing that eats other living things as food **(B43)**

contour plowing [kon′tōōr plou′ing] A type of plowing for growing crops; creates rows of crops around the sides of a hill instead of up and down **(C76)**

core [kôr] The center of the Earth **(C8)**

crust [krust] The solid outside layer of the Earth **(C8)**

deciduous forest [dē•sij′ōō•əs fôr′ist] A forest in which most of the trees lose and regrow their leaves each year **(B13)**

decomposer [dē′kəm•pōz′er] A living thing that breaks down dead organisms for food **(B44)**

desert [dez′ərt] An ecosystem where there is very little rain **(B20)**

earthquake [ûrth′kwāk′] The shaking of Earth's surface caused by movement of the crust and mantle **(C48)**

ecosystem [ek′ō•sis′təm] The living and non-living things in an environment **(B7)**

energy [en′ər•jē] The ability to cause change **(F6)**

energy pyramid [en′ər•jē pir′ə•mid] A diagram that shows that the amount of useable energy in an ecosystem is less for each higher animal in the food chain **(B50)**

environment [in•vī′rən•mənt] The things, both living and nonliving, that surround a living thing **(B6)**

erosion [i•rō′zhən] The movement of weathered rock and soil **(C42)**

estuary [es′chōō•er′•ē] A place where fresh water from a river mixes with salt water from the ocean **(D12)**

evaporation [ē•vap′ə•rā′shən] The process by which a liquid changes into a gas **(D17, E18)**

fish [fish] An animal that lives its whole life in water and breathes with gills **(A52)**

flood [flud] A large amount of water that covers normally dry land **(C50)**

food chain [fōōd′ chān′] The path of food from one living thing to another **(B48)**

food web [fōōd′ web′] A model that shows how food chains overlap **(B54)**

force [fôrs] A push or a pull **(F58)**

forest [fôr′ist] An area in which the main plants are trees **(B12)**

fossil [fos′əl] Something that has lasted from a living thing that died long ago **(C20)**

fresh water [fresh′ wôt′ər] Water that has very little salt in it **(B26)**

front [frunt] A place where two air masses of different temperatures meet **(D37)**

gas [gas] A form of matter that does not have a definite shape or a definite volume **(E12)**

germinate [jûr′mə•nāt′] When a new plant breaks out of the seed **(A13)**

gills [gilz] A body part found in fish and young amphibians that takes in oxygen from the water **(A51)**

glacier [glā′shər] A huge sheet of ice **(C44)**

gravity [grav′i•tē] The force that pulls objects toward each other **(F62)**

groundwater [ground′wôt′ər] A form of fresh water that is found under Earth's surface **(D8)**

habitat [hab′ə•tat′] The place where a population lives in an ecosystem **(B7)**

heat [hēt] The movement of thermal energy from one place to another **(F8)**

humus [hyōō′məs] The part of the soil made up of decayed parts of once-living things **(C62)**

igneous rock [ig′nē•əs rok′] A rock that was once melted rock but has cooled and hardened **(C12)**

inclined plane [in•klīnd′ plān′] A simple machine made of a flat surface set at an angle to another surface **(F71)**

inexhaustible resource [in′eg•zôs′tə•bəl rē′sôrs] A resource such as air or water that can be used over and over and can't be used up **(C94)**

inherit [in•her′it] To receive traits from parents **(A38)**

insulator [in′sə•lāt′ər] A material in which thermal energy does not move easily **(F15)**

interact [in′tər•akt′] When plants and animals affect one another or the environment to meet their needs **(B42)**

landform [land′fôrm′] A natural shape or feature of Earth's surface **(C34)**

leaf [lēf] A plant part that grows out of the stem; it takes in the air and light that a plant needs **(A7)**

lever [lev′ər] A bar that moves on or around a fixed point **(F70)**

liquid [lik′wid] A form of matter that has volume that stays the same, but can change its shape **(E12)**

loam [lōm] A type of topsoil that is rich in minerals and has lots of humus **(C70)**

lunar eclipse [loo′nər i•klips′] The hiding of the moon when it passes through the Earth's shadow **(D78)**

mammal [mam′əl] An animal that has fur or hair and is fed milk from its mother's body **(A42)**

mantle [man′təl] The middle layer of the Earth **(C8)**

mass [mas] The amount of matter in an object **(E24)**

matter [mat′ər] Anything that takes up space **(E6)**

metamorphic rock [met′ə•môr′fik rok′] A rock that has been changed by heat and pressure **(C12)**

mineral [min′ər•əl] An object that is solid, is formed in nature, and has never been alive **(C6)**

mixture [miks′chər] A substance that contains two or more different types of matter **(E41)**

motion [mō′shən] A change in position **(F59)**

mountain [moun′tən] A landform; a place on Earth's surface that is much higher than the land around it **(C35)**

nonrenewable resource [non′ri•noo′ə•bəl rē′sôrs] A resource, such as coal or oil, that will be used up someday **(C96)**

orbit [ôr′bit] The path an object takes as it moves around another object in space **(D58)**

phases [fāz•əz] The different shapes the moon seems to have in the sky when observed from Earth **(D76)**

photosynthesis [fōt′ō•sin′thə•sis] The food-making process of plants **(A20)**

physical change [fiz′i•kəl chānj] A change to matter in which no new kinds of matter are formed **(E40)**

physical property [fiz′i•kəl prop′ər•tē] Anything you can observe about an object by using your senses **(E6)**

plain [plān] A landform; a flat area on Earth's surface **(C35)**

planet [plan′it] A large body of rock or gas that orbits the sun **(D58)**

plateau [pla•tō′] A landform; a flat area higher than the land around it **(C35)**

population [pop′yōō•lā′shən] A group of the same kind of living thing that all live in one place at the same time **(B7)**

precipitation [prē•sip′ə•tā′shən] The water that falls to Earth as rain, snow, sleet, or hail **(D18)**

predator [pred′ə•tər] An animal that hunts another animal for food **(B54)**

prey [prā] An animal that is hunted by a predator **(B54)**

prism [priz′əm] A solid, transparent object that bends light into colors **(F44)**

producer [prə•dōōs′ər] A living thing that makes its own food **(B43)**

recycle [rē•si′kəl] To reuse a resource to make something new **(C100)**

reflection [ri•flek′shən] The bouncing of light off an object **(F36)**

refraction [ri•frak′shən] The bending of light when it moves from one kind of matter to another **(F38)**

renewable resource [ri•nōō′ə•bəl rē′sôrs] A resource that can be replaced in a human lifetime **(C94)**

reptile [rep′tīl] A land animal that has dry skin covered by scales **(A55)**

resource [rē′sôrs] A material that is found in nature and that is used by living things **(C88)**

revolution [rev′ə•lōō′shən] The movement of one object around another object **(D68)**

rock [rok] A solid made of minerals **(C8)**

rock cycle [rok′ si′kəl] The process in which one type of rock changes into another type of rock **(C14)**

root [rōōt] The part of a plant that holds the plant in the ground and takes in water and minerals from the soil **(A7)**

rotation [rō•tā′shən] The spinning of an object on its axis **(D68)**

S

salt water [sôlt′ wôt′ər] Water that has a lot of salt in it **(B26)**

scales [skālz] The small, thin, flat plates that help protect the bodies of fish and reptiles **(A52)**

sedimentary rock [sed′ə•men′tər•ē rok′] A rock formed from material that has settled into layers and been squeezed until it hardens into rock **(C12)**

seed [sēd] The first stage in the growth of many plants **(A12)**

seedling [sēd′ling] A young plant **(A13)**

simple machine [sim′pəl mə•shēn′] A tool that helps people do work **(F70)**

soil [soil] The loose material in which plants can grow in the upper layer of Earth **(C62)**

solar eclipse [sō′lər i•klips′] The hiding of the sun that occurs when the moon passes between the sun and Earth **(D80)**

solar system [sō′lər sis′təm] The sun and the objects that orbit around it **(D58)**

solid [sol′id] A form of matter that takes up a specific amount of space and has a definite shape **(E11)**

solution [sə•lōō′shən] A mixture in which the particles of two different kinds of matter mix together evenly **(E42)**

speed [spēd] The measure of how fast something moves over a certain distance **(F61)**

star [stär] A hot ball of glowing gases, like our sun **(D84)**

stem [stem] A plant part that connects the roots with the leaves of a plant and supports the plant above ground; it carries water from the roots to other parts of the plant **(A7)**

strip cropping [strip′ krop′ing] A type of planting that uses strips of thick grass or clover between strips of crops **(C76)**

T

telescope [tel′ə•skōp′] An instrument used to see faraway objects **(D88)**

temperature [tem′pər•ə•chər] The measure of how hot or cold something is **(D36)**

thermal energy [thûr′məl en′ər•jē] The energy that moves the particles in matter **(F7)**

thermometer [thûr•mom′ə•tər] A tool used to measure temperature **(F20)**

topsoil [top′soil′] The top layer of soil made up of the smallest grains and the most humus **(C63)**

trait [trāt] A body feature that an animal inherits; it can also be some things that an animal does **(A38)**

tropical rain forest [trop′i•kəl rān′fôr′ist] A hot, wet forest where the trees grow very tall and their leaves stay green all year **(B14)**

valley [val′ē] A landform; a lowland area between higher lands, such as mountains **(C35)**

volcano [vol•kā′nō] An opening in Earth's surface from which lava flows **(C49)**

volume [vol′yo͞om] The amount of space that matter takes up **(E22)**

water cycle [wôt′ər sī′kəl] The movement of water from Earth's surface into the air and back to the surface again **(D19)**

weather [weth′ər] The happenings in the atmosphere at a certain time **(D32)**

weather map [weth′ər map′] A map that shows weather data for a large area **(D46)**

weathering [weth′ər•ing] The process by which rock is worn down and broken apart **(C40)**

weight [wāt] The measure of the pull of gravity on an object **(F62)**

wind [wind] The movement of air **(D40)**

work [wûrk] The measure of force that it takes to move an object a certain distance **(F66)**

Photography Credits - Page placement key: (t) top, (c) center, (b) bottom, (l) left, (r) right, (bg) background, (i) inset

Cover Background, Charles Krebs/Tony Stone Images; Inset, Jody Dole.

Unit A - A1 (bg) Thomas Brase/Tony Stone Images; (i) Denis Valentine/The Stock Market; A2-A3 (bg) Joe McDonald/Bruce Coleman; A3 (i) Marilyn Kazmers/Deminsky Photo Associates; A4 Ed Young/AGStock USA; A6 (l) Anthony Edgeworth/The Stock Market; (r) Chris Vincent/The Stock Market; A6-A7 (bg) Barbara Gerlach/Dembinsky Photo Associates; A7 (c) Wendy W. Cortesi; A8 (t) Runk/Schoenberger/Grant Heilman Photography; (c) Runk/Schoenberger/Grant Heilman Photography; (bl) Renee Lynn/Photo Researchers; (br) Dr. E. R. Degginger/Color-Pic; A9 Runk/Schoenberger/Grant Heilman Photography; A10 Runk/Schoenberger/Grant Heilman Photography; A12 (l) Bonnie Sue/Grant Heilman/Photo Researchers; (r) Klaus Paysan/Peter Arnold, Inc.; (r) Runk/Schoenberger/Grant Heilman Photography; (ri) Runk/Schoenberger/Grant Heilman Photography; A13 (tr) Ed Young/AGStock USA; (b) Dr. E. R. Degginger/Color-Pic; A14 (tr) Richard Shiell/Dembinsky Photo Associates; (bl) Robert Carr/Bruce Coleman, Inc.; (br) Scott Sinklier/AGStock USA; A16 (t) Thomas D. Mangelsen/Peter Arnold, Inc.; (c) E.R. Degginger/Natural Selection Stock Photography; (bl) Randall B. Henne/Dembinsky Photo Associates; (br) Stan Osolinski/Dembinsky Photo Associates; (l) Scott Camazine/Photo Researchers; A17 William Harlow/Photo Researchers; A18 Christi Carter/Grant Heilman Photography; A20 Runk/Schoenberger/Grant Heilman Photography; A22 (t) DiMaggio/Kalish/The Stock Market; (cl) Jan-Peter Lahall/Peter Arnold, Inc.; (br) Holt Studios/Nigel Cattlin/Photo Researchers; A23 Robert Carr/Bruce Coleman; A24 Richard Shiell; A25 J. Sapinsky/The Stock Market; A26 (tr) Corbis; A30-A31 (bkgd) Art Wolfe/Tony Stone Images; A31 (cr) Astrid & Hanns Frieder Michler/Science Photo Library/Photo Researchers; A32 (bl) Rosemary Calvert/Tony Stone Images; (l) Ralph A. Reinhold/Animals Animals; (2) Johnny Johnson/ Tony Stone Images; (3) Mike Severns/ Tom Stack & Associates; (4) Fred Whitehead/Animals Animals; (5) Art Wolfe/ Tony Stone Images; (6) J.C. Stevenson/Animals Animals; A34-A35 Doug Perrine/Innerspace Visions; A35 (t) Ronald Hellstrom/Bruce Coleman, Inc.; (br) Stan Osolinski/Tony Stone Images; A36 (t) Mike Severns/Tony Stone Images; (lc) Kevin Schafer Photography; (bl) Marilyn Kazmers/Peter Arnold, Inc.; (br) Karen Su/Tony Stone Images; A38 (t) Rudie Kuiter/Innerspace Visions; (c) Fred Bruemmer/Peter Arnold, Inc.; (b) Art Wolfe/Tony Stone Images; A39 Phil A. Dotson/Photo Researchers; A40 Brian Stablyk/Tony Stone Images; A43 (t) Paul Metzger/Photo Researchers; (b) Frans Lanting/Minden Pictures; A44 (t) Stephen Dalton/Photo Researchers; (c) Tom McHugh/Photo Researchers; (b) Evelyn Gallardo/Peter Arnold, Inc.; (cl) The Photo Library-Sydney/Gary Lewis/Photo Researchers; (br) Francois Gohier/Photo Researchers; A45 (t) Theo Allofs/Tony Stone Images; (blue jay) Wayne Lankinen/Bruce Coleman, Inc.; (macaw) M. Mastrorillo/The Stock Market; (emperor penguin) Kjell B. Sandved/Photo Researchers; (ostrich) Leonard Lee Rue III/Photo Researchers; (bee humming bird) Robert A. Tyrrell Photography; (peacock) Tom McHugh/Photo Researchers; A46 (t) Manfred Danegger/Tony Stone Images; (cl) John Cancalosi/Peter Arnold, Inc.; (b) Bill Ivy/Tony Stone Images; (br) Stan Osolinski/The Stock Market; A48 (c) O.S.F./ Animals Animals; (b) Tim Davis/Tony Stone Images; A50 (tl) Nuridsany et Perennou/Photo Researchers; (r) E.R. Degginger/Photo Researchers; (bl) Joseph T. Collins/Photo Researchers; A52 (t) David M. Schleser/Nature's Images; (c) Andrea & Antonella Ferrari/Innerspace Visions; A52-A53 Kelvin Aitken/Peter Arnold, Inc.; A53 (t) Zig Leszczynski/Animals Animals; (c) Kelvin Aitken/Peter Arnold, Inc.; (br) Tom McHugh/Steinhart Aquarium/Photo Researchers; A54(tr) Kim Taylor/Bruce Coleman, Inc.; (c) Fred Bavendam/Minden Pictures; (b) Fred Bavendam/Minden Pictures; A55 (t) Zig Leszczynski/Animals Animals; (b) Suzanne L. Collins & Joseph T. Collins/Photo Researchers; (bli) Dwight R. Kuhn; A56 (t) Jany Sauvanet/Photo Researchers; (c) G.E. Schmida/Fritz/Bruce Coleman, Inc.; A56-A57 (t) Tom & Pat Leeson/Photo Researchers; A57 Schafer & Hill/Tony Stone Images; A58 (t) Tom Brakefield/Bruce Coleman, Inc.; (c) Dr. E. R. Degginger/Color-Pic; (b) Michael Holford; A59 Emory Kristof/National Geographic Image Collection; A60 (tr) Bertha G. Gomez; (bl) Michael Fogden/bruce Coleman, Inc.

Unit B - B1 (bg) Derek Redfeam/The Image Bank; (i) George E. Stewart/Dembinsky Photo Association; B2-B3 (bg) Sven Linoblad/Photo Researchers; B2 (i) Wayne P. Armstrong; B4 Hans Pfletschinger/Peter Arnold, Inc.; B6 (l) Dwight R. Kuhn; (r) Michael Durham/ENP Images; B7 Frank Krahmer/Bruce Coleman, Inc.; B8 (tl) Jeff and Alexa Henry/Peter Arnold, Inc.; (t) Jeff and Alexa Henry/Peter Arnold, Inc.; (b) Christoph Burki/Tony Stone Images; B10 Kennan Ward/The Stock Market; B13 (all) James P. Jackson/Photo Researchers; B14 Zefa Germany/The Stock Market; B15 Janis Burger/Bruce Coleman Inc.; B16 (r) Michael Quinton/Minden Pictures; B16-B17 (b)Grant Heilman Photography; B18 J.C. Carton/Bruce Coleman, Inc.; B20 (l) Wolfgang Kaehler Photography; (r) James Randklev/Tony Stone Images; B21 Dr. E.R. Degginger/Color-Pic; B22 (l) Paul Chesley/Tony Stone Images; (r) Jeff Foott/Bruce Coleman, Inc.; (i) Jen & Des Bartlett/Bruce Coleman, Inc.; B23 Lee Rentz/Bruce Coleman, Inc.; B24 Leo De Wys Inc.; B27 (li) R.N. Mariscal/Bruce Coleman, Inc.; (b) Dr. E.R. Degginger/Color-Pic; (r) Naitar E. Harvey, APSA/National Audubon Society/Photo Researchers; B28 Flip Nicklin/Minden Pictures; B29 (t) Norbert Wu/Peter Arnold, Inc.; (b) Norbert Wu/Peter Arnold, Inc.; B30 (t) Gary Meszaros/Bruce Coleman, Inc.; (bli) Stevan Stefanovic/Okapia/Photo Researchers; (bci) Dwight R. Kuhn; (br) Phil Degginger/Color-Pic; B30-B31 (b) Jeff Greenberg/Photo Researchers; B32 (t) Courtesy of Jane Weaver/Parie Project/L. A. Gililand Elementary; (ti) Globe-NASA/ Goddard Scientific Visualization Studio; B33 Derke/O'Hara/Tony Stone Images; B34 (t) The Marjorie N. Boyer Trust; (bl) Anthony Mercieca/ Parie Project/B38-B39 Luiz C. Marigo/Peter Arnold, Inc.; B39 (br) Roland Seitre/Peter Arnold, Inc.; B40 (l) Roy Morsch/The Stock Market; (c) Norbert Wu/Tony Stone Images; (r) Rosemary Calvert/Tony Stone Images; B41 (bl) Stan Osolinski/The Stock Market; (c) R. Kopfle/KOPFL/Bruce Coleman; (br) Michael Durham/ENP Images; (b) Hans Reinhard/Bruce Coleman, Inc.; (li) Dwight R. Kuhn; (ri) Dr. Paul A. Zahl/Photo Researchers; B42 (t) Wolfgang Kaehler Photography; (b) Rob Hadlow/Bruce Coleman, Inc.; B44 (t) Stephen Dalton/Photo Researchers; (c) Andrew Syred/Science Photo Library/Photo Researchers; (b) Stephen Krasemann/Tony Stone Images; B46 Laurie Campbell/Tony Stone Images; B48 Dwight R. Kuhn; B49 (t) Paul E. Taylor/Photo Researchers; (c) Holt Studios/Photo Researchers; B50 (r) Breck P. Kent/Animals Animals; B51 Mitsuaki Iwago/Minden Pictures; B52 Erwin and Peggy Bauer/Bruce Coleman, Inc.; B54-B55 Michael Durham/ENP Images; B57 Jane Burton/Bruce Coleman, Inc.; B58 (cl) LASCAUX Caves II, France/Explorer, Paris/Superstock; (c) Fred Bruemmer/Peter Arnold; (cb) Tom Brakefield/Bruce Coleman; B60 (tl) Leah Edelstein-Keshet/University of British Columbia; (bl) Fred McConnaughey/Photo Researchers.

Unit C Other - C1(bg) Richard Price/FPG International; (i) Martin Land/Science Photo Library/Photo Researchers; C2-C3 (bg) E. R. Degginger; C2 (bc) A. J. Copley/Visuals Unlimited; C3 (ri) Paul Chesley/Tony Stone Images; C4 (b) The Natural History Museum, London; C6 (tl), (ct), (cb) Dr. E. R. Degginger/Color-Pic; (r) E. R. Degginger/Bruce Coleman, Inc.; (bl) Mark A. Schneider/Dembinsky Photo Associates; C6-C7 (b) Chromosohm/Joe Sohm/Photo Researchers; C7 (tr) Blair Seitz/Photo Researchers; (tri), (bli) Dr. E. R. Degginger/Color-Pic; C8 (t) Barry Runk/Grant Heilman Photography; (ct) Dr. E. R. Degginger/Color-Pic; (b) Dr. E. R. Degginger/Color-Pic; (cb) Barry L. Runk/Grant Heilman Photography; C8-9 (t) Robert Pettit/Dembinsky Photo Associates; C10 Tom Bean/Tom & Susan Bean, Inc.; C12 Jim Steinberg/Photo Researchers; C12-C13 (b) G. Brad Lewis/Photo Resource Hawaii; C14 (l), (tr) Dr. E. R. Degginger/Color-Pic; C14 (br) Aaron Haupt/Photo Researchers; C15 (tl) Robert Pettit/Dembinsky Photo Associates; (tr) Charles R. Belinky/Photo Researchers; (bl), (bc), (br) Dr. E. R. Degginger/Color-Pic; C16 (t) Roger Du Buisson/The Stock Market; (c) Jay Mallin Photos; C16-C17 (b) Ed Wheeler/The Stock Market; C18 Stephen Wilkes/The Image Bank; C21 (t) William E. Ferguson; (bl) Kerry T. Givens/Bruce Coleman, Inc.; (br) Joy Spurr/Bruce Coleman, Inc.; C22 (t) AP Photo/Dennis Cook; (b) M. Timothy O'Keefe/Bruce Coleman, Inc.; C24 (t) Francois Gohier/Photo Researchers; (b) The Natural History Museum/London; C25 Stan Osolinski; C26 (tr) Jean Miele/Lamont-Doherty Earth Observatory of Columbia University; C30-C31 (t) John Warden/Tony Stone Images; C31 (bl) Harold Naideau/The Stock Market; C32 (t) Dr. Alan Nelson/Dembinsky Photo Associates; C33 (b) Darrell Gulin/Dembinsky Photo Associates; C35 (t) Michael Hubrich/Dembinsky Photo Associates; (c) Mark E. Gibson; C36 (t) Breck P. Kent/Earth Scenes; C36-37 (b) Paraskevas Photography; C38 Mark E. Gibson; C40 (bl) Dr. E.R. Degginger/Color-Pic; C40 (bc) Mark A. Schneider/Dembinsky Photo Associates; C40-C41 (br-b) Rod Planck/Dembinsky Photo Associates; (c) John Gerlach/Dembinsky Photo Associates; C42 (t) Georg Gerster/Photo Researchers; (c) NASA Photo/Grant Heilman Photography; C42-C43 (b) C.C. Lockwood/Earth Scenes; C43 (t)

Mark E. Gibson; C46 Ken Sakamoto/Black Star; C48 (l) David Parker/SPL/Photo Researchers; (l) AP/Wide World Photos; C49 (l) AP/Wide World Photos; (r) AP Photo/Wide World Photos; (bl) Will & Deni McIntyre/Photo Researchers; C50-C51 AP/Wide World Photos; C52 (l) George Hall/Woodfin Camp & Associates; (i) Laura Riley/Bruce Coleman; C53 J. Aronovsky/Zuma Images/The Stock Market; C54 (tr) Courtesy of Scott Rowland; (bl) Dennis Oda/Tony Stone Images; C58-C59 (bg) Lynn M. Stone/Bruce Coleman, Inc.; C59 (br) NASA; C60 Ann Duncan/Tom Stack & Associates; C63 (all) Bruce Coleman, Inc.; C66 Grant Heilman/Grant Heilman Photography; C68-C69 (b) Gary Irving/Panoramic Images; C68 (l) Barry L. Runk/Grant Heilman Photography; C69 (li), (r) Barry L. Runk/Grant Heilman Photography; C70-C71 (b) Larry Lefever/Grant Heilman Photography; C72 Andy Sacks/Tony Stone Images; C74 USDA - Soil Conservation Service; C74-C75 (b) Dr. E. R. Degginger/Color-Pic; C75 (t) James D. Nations/D. Donne Bryant; (tli) Gunter Ziseler/Peter Arnold, Inc.; (tri) S.A.M./Wolfgang Kaehler Photography; (bli) Walter H. Hodge/Peter Arnold, Inc.; (bri) Jim Steinberg/Photo Researchers; C76 (t) Thomas Hovland from Grant Heilman Photography; (b) B.W. Hoffmann/AGStock USA; C78 (b) Randall B. Henne/Dembinsky Photo Associates; (l) Russ Munn/AgStock USA; C79 Bruce Hands/Tony Stone Images; C80 (t) Courtesy of Diana Wall, Colorado State University; (bl) Oliver Mickes/Ottawa/Photo Researchers; C84-C85 (bg) Kirby, Richar OSF/Earth Scenes; C86 Bob Daemmrich/Bob Daemmrich Photography, Inc.; C88 (l) Peter Correz/Tony Stone Images; (c) Mark E. Gibson; C88-C89(b) Bill Lea/Dembinsky Photo Associates; C90 (t) Chris Rogers/Rainbow/PNI; (r) Yoav Levy/Phototake/PNI; C91 Rob Badger Photography; C92 (bl) Christie's Images, London/Superstock; (br) Jeff Greenberg / Photo Researchers; (bc) Joyce Photographics / Photo Researchers; (tr) Mary Ann Kulla/ The Stock Market; C93 (t) Alan L. Detrick / Photo Researchers; (bc) Archive Photos; (br) David Barnes /The Stock Market; (bl) Gary Retherford/ Photo Researchers; C94-C95 Jeff Greenberg/Visuals Unlimited; C95 (tl) Wolfgang Fischer/Peter Arnold, Inc.; (tr) Wolfgang Fischer/Peter Arnold, Inc.; (c) Craig Hammell/The Stock Market; C96 (t) Barbara Gerlach/Dembinsky Photo Associates; (b) Brownie Harris/The Stock Market; C97 Chris Rogers/The Stock Market; C98 Michael A. Keller/The Stock Market; C100-C101 (b) Ray Pfortner/Peter Arnold, Inc.; C103 William E. Ferguson; C104-C105 Blaine Harrington III/The Stock Market; C106 James King-Holmes/Science Photo Library/ Photo Researchers; C107 (bl) Wellman Fibers Industry; (r) Gabe Palmer/The Stock Market; C108 (tr) Susan Sterner/HRW; (bl) Kristin Finnegan/Tony Stone Images.

Unit D Other - D1(bg) Pal Hermansen/Tony Stone Images; (i) Earth Imaging/Tony Stone Images; D2-D3 (bg) Zefa Germany/The Stock Market; D3 (tr) Michael A. Keller/The Stock Market; (br) Steven Needham/Envision; D4 J. Shaw/Bruce Coleman, Inc.; D5 (b) NASA; D6 (l) Yu Somov; S. Korytnikov/Sovfoto/Eastfoto/PNI; (r) Christopher Arend/Alaska Stock Images/PNI; D7 Grant Heilman Photography; D8-D9 Dr. Eckart Pott/Bruce Coleman, Inc.; D10 N.R. Rowan/The Image Works; D12-D13 Mike Price/Bruce Coleman, Inc.; D13 David Job/Tony Stone Images; D14 John Beatty/Tony Stone Images; D17 (l) Grant Heilman Photography; (r) Darrell Gulin/Tony Stone Images; D20 NASA; D21 Ben Osborne/Tony Stone Images; D22 (t) Polytechnic State University; (b) NASA; D26-D27 Andrea Booher/Tony Stone Images; D27 NASA/Science Photo Library/Photo Researchers; D28 Joe Towers/The Stock Market; D30 Rich Iwasaki/Tony Stone Images; D32 (t) Peter Arnold; (c) Warren Faidley/International Stock Photography; (r) Stephen Simpson/FPG International; D33 E.R. Degginger/Bruce Coleman, Inc.; D34 Ray Pfortner/Peter Arnold, Inc.; D37 (t) Ralph H. Wetmore, II/Tony Stone Images; (b) Joe McDonald/Earth Scenes; D38 (c) Tom Bean; (b) Adam Jones/Photo Researchers; D42 Warren Faidley/International Stock Photography; D44 (l) Superstock; (r) David Ducros/Science Photo Library/Photo Researchers; D45 (both) © 1998 AccuWeather; D48 New Scientist Magazine; D49 Dwayne Newton/PhotoEdit; D50 (tr) Courtesy June Bacon-Bercey; (bl) David R. Frazier/Photo Researchers; D54-D55 David Hardy/Science Photo Library/Photo Researchers; D55 (tc) European Space Agency/Science Photo Library/Photo Researchers; D60 (t) U.S. Geological Survey/Science Photo Library/Photo Researchers; D60 (b) NASA; D60, D61, D62 (bg) Jerry Schad/Photo Researchers; D61 (t) National Oceanic and Atmospheric Administration; D61 (b) David Crisp and the WFPC2 Science Team (Jet Propulsion Laboratory/California Institute of Technology); D62 (t), (b) NASA; D63 (t) Erich Karkoschka (University of Arizona Lunar & Planetary Lab) and NASA; (c) NASA; (b) Nasa/Science Source/Photo Researchers; D64 J. Spurr/Bruce Coleman, Inc.; D65 Royer, Ronald/Science Photo Library/Photo Researchers; D66 Renee Lynn/Photo Researchers; D69 (l) Dr. E. R. Degginger/Color-Pic; (r) Dr. E. R. Degginger/Color-Pic; D72 (t) Joseph Nettis/Photo Researchers; (b) John Elk III/Bruce Coleman, Inc.; D74 NASA; D77 (all) Telegraph Colour Library/FPG International; D78-D79 Margaret Miller/Photo Researchers; D79 (t) Pekka Parviainen/Science Photo Library/Photo Researchers; (b) George East/Science Photo Library/Photo Researchers; D80 Dr. Fred Espenak/Science Photo Library/Photo Researchers; D82 The Granger Collection, New York; D88 Merritt Vincent/PhotoEdit; D90 (l) Rob Talbot/ Tony Stone Images; (r) Stephen Graham/Dembinsky Photo Associates; D91 NASA; D92 (both) NASA.

Unit E Other - E1(bg) Steve Barnett/Liaison International; (i) StockFood America/Lieberman; E2-E3 Chris Noble/Tony Stone Images; E3 Kent & Donna Dannen; E6 John Michael/International Stock Photography; E7 (r) R. Van Nostrand/Tony Stone Images; E8 (tr) Mike Timo/Tony Stone Images; E9 (t) Daniel J. Cox/Tony Stone Images; (ti) Goknar/Vogue/Superstock; E10 (br) John Michael/International Stock Photography; (bl) William Cornett/Image Excellence Photography; E11 (tr) Lee Foster/FPG International; (br) Paul Silverman/Fundamental Photographs; E12 (t) William Johnson/Stock, Boston; E12-E13 (b) Robert Finken/Photo Researchers; E14 S.J. Krasemann/Peter Arnold, Inc.; E16 (ri) Dr. E. R. Degginger/Color-Pic; E17 (l) Charles D. Winters/Photo Researchers; (r) Spencer Gran/PhotoEdit; E18-E19 Peter French/Pacific Stock; E20 J. Sebo/Zoo Atlanta; E25 (cr) Robert Pearcy/Animals Animals; E25 (cl) Ron Kimball Photography; E26 (tr) Jim Harrison/Stock, Boston; E32 (tr) Corbis; (bl) Alfred Pasieka/Science Photo Library/Photo Researchers; E36-E37 (bg)Dr. Dennis Kunkel/Phototake; E38 Robert Ginn/PhotoEdit; E42 (tl), (tr) Dr. E. R. Degginger/Color-Pic; (bl) Tom Pantages; (br) Tom Pantages; E44 Chip Clark; E44 (l) Tom Pantages; (r), (c) Tom Pantages; E47 (br) John Lund/Tony Stone Images; E50 John Gaudio; E51 Michael Newman/Photo Edit; E52 (tr) Los Alamos National Laboratory/Photo Researchers; (bl) US Army White Sands Missile Range.

Unit F - F1 (bg) Simon Fraser/Science Photo Library/Photo Researchers; (i) Nance Trueworthy/Liaison International; F2 (bg) April Rehm; (tr) M. W. Black/Bruce Coleman, Inc.; F6 (bl) Mary Kate Denny/PhotoEdit; (br) Gary A. Conner/PhotoEdit; F7 (b) Camerique, Inc./The Picture Cube; (br) Stephen Saks/The Picture Cube; F8 (cr) Pat Field/Bruce Coleman, Inc.; (bl) Mark E. Gibson; F9 (t) Dr. E.R. Degginger/Color-Pic; (r)Ryan and Beyer/Allstock/PNI; F10 (b) John Running/Stock, Boston; (cl) Joseph Nettis/Photo Researchers; F11 (t) Jeff Schultz/Alaska Stock Images; F16 (r) Buck Ennis/Stock, Boston; (b) J.C. Carton/Bruce Coleman, Inc.; F21 (t) Michael Holford Photographs; (br) Spencer Grant/PhotoEdit; F25 Marco Cristofori/ The Stock Market; F26 (tr) Corbis; (bc) Shaun Egan/Tony Stone Images; F30-F31 (bg) Jerry Lodriguss/Photo Researchers; F31 (br) Picture PerfectUSA; F32 (b) James M. Mejuto Photography; F34 (bl) Mark E. Gibson; (br) Bob Daemmrich/Stock, Boston; F35 (b) Myrleen Ferguson/PhotoEdit; F37 (b), (tl) Jan Butchofsky/Dave G. Houser; F39 (tr), (c) Richard Megna/Fundamental Photographs; F42 (b) Randy Duchaine/The Stock Market; F44 (t) Tom Skrivan/The Stock Market; F45 (tr) David Woodfall/Tony Stone Images; F47 (t) Roy Morsh/The Stock Market; F48 (l) Ed Eckstein for The Franklin Institute Science Museum; F49 (tr) Peter Angelo Simon/The Stock Market; F48-F49 Paul Silverman/ Fundamental Photography; F54-F55 (bg) Superstock; (br) David Madison/Bruce Coleman, Inc.; F58 (cl) John Running/Stock, Boston; (bch) David Young-Wolff/PhotoEdit; F59 H. Mark Weidman; F60 (t) D & I McDonald/The Picture Cube; F62 (b) Nasa/The Stock Market; (r) Richard Megna/Fundamental Photographs; F64 (b) Edith G. Haun/Stock, Boston; F70 (b) Amy C. Etra/PhotoEdit; F71 (t) Tony Freeman/PhotoEdit; F72 (b) Dave G. Houser; F74 Webb Chappell; F75 John Lei/Omni-Photo Communications; F76 (tr) NASA/Langley Research Center; (bl) Valder/Tormey/International Stock.

Health Handbook - R15 Palm Beach Post; R19 (tr) Andrew Speilman/Phototake; (c) Martha McBride/Unicorn; (br) Larry West/FPG International; R21 Superstock; R26 (c) Index Stock; R27 (tl) Renne Lynn/ Tony Stone Images; (tr) David Young-Wolff/PhotoEdit.

All Other photographs by Harcourt photographers listed below, © Harcourt:
Weronica Ankarorn, Bartlett Digital Photography, Victoria Bowen, Eric Camdem, Digital Imaging Group, Charles Hodges, Ken Karp, Ken Kinzie, Ed McDonald, Sheri O'Neal, Terry Sinclair.

Illustration Credits - Craig Austin A53; Graham Austin B56; John Butler A42; Rick Courtney A20, A51, B14, B55, C22, C40, C41, C62, C64; Mike Dammer A27, A61, B35, B61, C27, C55, C81, C109, D23, D51, D93, E35, E53, F27, F51, F77; Dennis Davidson D58; John Edwards D9, D17, D18, D31, D37, D39, D40, D59, D64, D68, D69, D70, D71, D76, D77, D78, D80, E17, D10, F45, F60; Wendy Griswold-Smith A37; Lisa Frasier F78; Geosystems C36, C42, C44, C103, D12, D46; Wayne Hovice B28; Tom Powers C8, C13, C20, C34, C50, C102; John Rice D16, B7, B21, B50; Ruttle D36, D7; Rosie Saunders A15; Shough C90, F22, F46, F71, F72.